Reasoning with Democratic Values

ETHICAL PROBLEMS IN UNITED STATES HISTORY

Reasoning with Democratic Values

ETHICAL PROBLEMS IN UNITED STATES HISTORY

Instructor's Manual

Alan L. Lockwood
University of Wisconsin
Madison, Wisconsin

David E. Harris
Oakland Schools
Pontiac, Michigan

Teachers College, Columbia University
New York and London

Published by Teachers College Press, 1234 Amsterdam Avenue, New York, N.Y. 10027

ISBN 0-8077-6101-X

Manufactured in the United States of America

98 9 8 7 6

CONTENTS

About the Curriculum

RATIONALE AND GOALS

The *Reasoning with Democratic Values: Ethical Problems in United States History* curriculum represents a way of approaching one of the traditional goals of the social studies—the promotion of social responsibility. Although this general goal is widely acknowledged to be an aim for the social studies, careful efforts to create systematic curricular practices consistent with this goal have rarely been made. This curriculum is the result of one such rare effort.

Social responsibility encompasses more than the conventional focus of citizenship education. According to the conventional view of citizenship education, the relations of citizens to formal institutions of government are the focus of study. Teaching for social responsibility goes beyond this view and recognizes that value questions of rights and duties arise in a variety of contexts. We act in many roles. As citizens, family members, friends, neighbors, and workers, we confront situations that require us to decide what actions constitute responsible behavior and what actions do not.

The approach to social responsibility taken by this curriculum recognizes the complexity of responsible decision making. The approach is not aimed at indoctrinating students into some predetermined set of behaviors. Rather, it assumes general agreement on a set of democratic values (life, liberty, property, equality, etc.) that should be upheld and followed. Agreement on a set of values does not, however, go far in helping to identify responsible behavior in concrete circumstances. Values can conflict, and their meanings are not always clear. Honest debate about what constitutes responsible action is often called for. The episodes in this curriculum stimulate such debate.

Research by such cognitive-developmental psychologists as Lawrence Kohlberg has shown that properly led discussions of ethical problems can help students advance the quality of their reasoning. Fair and open discussions permit the natural development of more mature thought about value issues. Students' thinking becomes less self-centered, less a product of simple conformity to the views of those around them, and more attuned to the legal rights of others and the well-being of the society in which they live. Students who have the opportunity to engage in such discussions are more likely to develop mature ethical reasoning than those who do not. Ethically mature reasoners come to understand better the role of values in social circumstances and are better able to express coherent and well-justified points of view about responsible action.

Systematic, rational thought cannot solve all problems. It is, however, a prerequisite to taking obligations seriously, recognizing and respecting the legitimate rights of others, and acting responsibly.

Teaching for social responsibility does not require the creation of a separate course in the social studies curriculum. Existing United States history courses provide an appropriate place for students to explore the meaning of responsible judgment and action. There are several reasons why history is a suitable subject for this enterprise. First of all, history provides events that actually involve complex ethical issues. In examining these events, students can evaluate the thinking and actions of historical figures, thereby developing reasoning abilities that can be applied to current and future circumstances. Second, history presents events that are removed from students' daily lives. This remoteness allows for more dispassionate reflection about right and wrong. Judgments are less clouded by the bias and urgency that often hinder clear thinking about current situations, in which there may be personal and immediate emotional involvement. Finally, history demonstrates that conflict over ethical values is not transient. Differences of opinion regarding democratic values are historically persistent. Reflection about these matters is not a contemporary fad, but a recurring and pervasive theme of the United States' heritage.

Although chronologically organized, the curriculum is not a comprehensive survey of the scope of United States history. Rather, it is intended to supplement existing courses by providing episodes selected because they embody conflict over democratic values in their historical context. The democratic values are simply defined for this curriculum as:

AUTHORITY: a value concerning what rules or people should be obeyed and the consequences for disobedience

EQUALITY: a value concerning whether people should be treated in the same way

LIBERTY: a value concerning what freedoms people should have and the limits that may justifiably be placed on them

LIFE: a value concerning when, if ever, it is justifiable to threaten or take a life

LOYALTY: a value concerning obligations to the people, traditions, ideas, and organizations of importance in one's life

PROMISE-KEEPING: a value concerning the nature of duties that arise when promises are made

PROPERTY: a value concerning what people should be allowed to own and how they should be allowed to use it

TRUTH: a value concerning the expression, distortion, or withholding of accurate information

The principal aim of the discussion of value-laden historical events is the fostering of social responsibility. This curriculum is designed to accomplish a set of more specific goals as well. As a result of regular instruction from *Reasoning with Democratic Values*, students will

1. Develop more complex and systematic reasoning about decisions involving democratic values
2. Gain a deeper understanding of important events, people, and issues from the American past
3. Increase their ability to identify ethical values and to analyze situations involving them
4. Demonstrate increased respect for individual rights and responsibilities
5. Improve their ability to express clearly reasoned judgments, both orally and in writing
6. Become more effective participants in productive group discussions of ethical issues

CONTENT AND ORGANIZATION

Volumes 1 and 2 of *Reasoning with Democratic Values: Ethical Problems in United States History* are aimed primarily at students enrolled in secondary school courses in United States history. The reading level of the episodes, as assessed by the Dale-Chall Readability Formula, is appropriate for typical secondary students. Field testing indicates that these volumes can trigger stimulating discussions with adult groups as well.

There are seven chronological parts in the two volumes. Volume 1, containing three parts, covers 21 episodes, beginning with the colonial era and ending with the Reconstruction (1607–1876). Volume 2, containing four parts, covers 28 episodes, beginning with the era of expansion and reform (from 1877) and ending with problems that have faced Americans in the contemporary era. Each of these episodes characterizes an ethical problem that occurred in the era.

At the end of each of the episodes is a four-section sequence of activities.

The first section of the activities is called *Historical Understanding*. It poses questions that help students see the broader historical context from which the episode has been drawn. The second section of the activities, called *Reviewing the Facts of the Case*, contains more specific questions about the episode. These questions must be answered to discuss the episode in some depth.

The remaining two sections of the activities require students to employ higher-level thinking skills. The third section, *Analyzing Ethical Issues*, presents an exercise designed to sharpen students' ability to use analytical reasoning. Students are asked to distinguish factual from ethical issues, recognize particular democratic values embedded in the episode, explore the meaning of the democratic values, or identify conflicts among the values.

The final section of the activities, entitled *Expressing Your Reasoning*, requires evaluative reasoning by students. The questions posed in this section ask students to make judgments, orally or in writing, about right and wrong as they grapple with ethical issues raised by the episode.

A chart for each part briefly sketching the content of its seven episodes follows. The charts show the title and topic of each episode and the key democratic values raised in it.

QUESTIONS AND ANSWERS ABOUT THE CURRICULUM

When new social studies materials are published, teachers, administrators, parents, and others often raise questions about the teaching approach presented in the materials. This section includes questions that have been raised about the *Reasoning with Democratic Values* curriculum and gives brief responses by the authors.

Q. Is this curriculum a type of values education?

A. Yes. There are numerous approaches to handling value issues in classrooms. In the *Values Education Sourcebook*, Douglas Superka and colleagues at the Social Science Education Consortium identified six general types of values education: inculcation, moral development, analysis, evocation and union, clarification, and action learning. The approach taken by the *Reasoning with Democratic Values* curriculum resembles both analysis and moral development. Among other things, the latter approaches stress the application of rational thinking and discussion when dealing with ethical issues. Unlike those approaches, however, this curriculum has additional goals related to promoting deeper understanding and appreciation of United States history.

Q. I have heard of Values Clarification and understand that it has caused controversy in many schools around the nation. Is this curriculum a version of Values Clarification?

A. No. This curriculum is not a version of Values Clarification. In fact, one of the authors, Professor Alan Lockwood, has been a vigorous critic of Values Clarification. Values Clarification has been criticized for treating ethical value issues superficially, for tending to promote ethical relativism, for

(continued on page 14)

TOPIC AND VALUES CHART

EPISODE TITLE AND TOPIC	KEY DEMOCRATIC VALUES INVOLVED							
Volume 1, Part 1: The Colonial Era (1607–1776)	Authority	Equality	Liberty	Life	Loyalty	Promise-keeping	Property	Truth
1. Friends and Enemies *Mary Dyer's fight for religious freedom in Puritan New England*	X		X	X	X			
2. Madness in Massachusetts *Tensions and fears of witchcraft in Salem, Massachusetts during the 1690s*	X		X					X
3. Hatred on the Frontier *Hostility between whites and Indians in the western part of the Pennsylvania colony*	X	X		X		X	X	X
4. A Sticky Business *Smuggling as a cause of strain between England and the colonies*	X						X	X
5. Defending the Redcoats *John Adams' decision to defend the British soldiers accused in the Boston Massacre*	X		X	X	X			
6. From Triumph to Treason *Benedict Arnold's fall from hero to traitor*	X				X	X	X	
7. A Luxury We Can't Afford *Thomas Jefferson's struggle with slavery*	X	X					X	

(*continued*)

TOPIC AND VALUES CHART (*continued*)

EPISODE TITLE AND TOPIC	KEY DEMOCRATIC VALUES INVOLVED							
Volume 1, Part 2: The New Nation (1777–1850)	Authority	Equality	Liberty	Life	Loyalty	Promise-keeping	Property	Truth
1. The Desperate Debtors *Daniel Shays' rebellion against the government of Massachusetts*	X						X	
2. The Price of Free Speech *Attempts of the new national administration to restrict free expression during John Adams' presidency*	X	X	X		X	X		X
3. Denmark's Gamble in South Carolina *The attempt of Denmark Vesey to end slavery*	X	X	X	X	X		X	X
4. A Woman's Place Is in the Factory *The struggle of U.S. working women in the period of early industrialization*	X		X				X	X
5. An Unconquered Indian *The attempt of Seminole Chief Osceola to resist removal of his people from the Southeast*	X			X		X	X	X
6. The Collapse of Brotherly Love *Strife between Catholics and Protestants in Philadelphia in 1844*	X	X	X	X				X
7. A Different Drummer *Henry David Thoreau and his protest of the Mexican War*	X		X	X	X			

Volume 1, Part 3: A House Divided (1850–1876)	Authority	Equality	Liberty	Life	Loyalty	Promise-keeping	Property	Truth
1. You Can't Hold Still *The struggle of a slave, Peter Still, to buy himself*	X	X	X	X	X		X	X
2. Freemen to the Rescue *Defiance of the Fugitive Slave Law in Wisconsin*	X	X			X		X	
3. Quoth the Raven: No! No! No! *Sam Houston and the conflict over secession in Texas*	X	X	X		X			
4. Tears of Blood *Robert E. Lee's decision to resign from the U.S. Army*	X				X	X		
5. The Miseries of Dr. Mudd *Dr. Samuel Mudd's conviction and imprisonment for conspiring in the assassination of President Lincoln*	X	X	X	X	X			X
6. Pioneer Suffragist *Susan B. Anthony and the 1867 woman suffrage campaign in Kansas*	X	X		X	X		X	
7. The Beast and the "Bagger" *Civil rights during Reconstruction in Louisiana*	X	X	X	X	X	X	X	

(*continued*)

TOPIC AND VALUES CHART (*continued*)

EPISODE TITLE AND TOPIC	KEY DEMOCRATIC VALUES INVOLVED							
Volume 2, Part 1: Expansion and Reform (1877–1918)	Authority	Equality	Liberty	Life	Loyalty	Promise-keeping	Property	Truth
1. Reservations Not Accepted *The conflict between the U.S. government and Chief Joseph of the Nez Perce Indians over reservation policy*	X		X	X		X	X	
2. A Rare Medium *Controversy surrounding Victoria Woodhull's views of freedom*		X	X				X	X
3. The Maine Magnetic Man *Charges of political corruption surrounding James G. Blaine*		X			X	X	X	
4. A Simple Act of Justice *Illinois Governor John Peter Altgeld's pardon of the Haymarket anarchists*	X		X	X	X		X	
5. Throne Overthrown *The Hawaiian Revolution and annexation of Hawaii*	X	X			X			
6. Sinking Into War *William Jennings Bryan and the United States' entry into World War I*			X	X			X	X
7. Speaking His Peace *Eugene V. Debs' decision to speak out against World War I in violation of the Espionage Act*	X		X		X		X	

Volume 2, Part 2: Normalcy and Depression (1919–1940)	Authority	Equality	Liberty	Life	Loyalty	Promise-keeping	Property	Truth
1. Bay State Blues *The Boston Police strike of 1919 and the response of Massachusetts Governor Calvin Coolidge*	X		X		X		X	
2. Stealing North *The work experiences of Richard Wright as a black teenager in the "Jim Crow" South of the 1920s*	X	X	X		X	X	X	X
3. Rebel Without a Pause *The problems of Zelda Fitzgerald during the "Roaring Twenties"*	X		X				X	X
4. Bad News *Jay Near's newspaper tests the limits of freedom of the press in the case of* Near v. Minnesota	X		X		X	X		X
5. Soldiers of Misfortune *Conflict between the Bonus Army and federal authorities in Washington, D.C. during the Great Depression*	X	X	X	X	X			X
6. United We Sit *The General Motors sit-down strike of 1937 in Flint, Michigan and the response of Governor Frank Murphy*	X	X	X	X	X		X	
7. Yearning to Breathe Free *Jewish refugees from Nazi Germany seek admittance to the U.S. in exception to the U.S. immigration laws.*	X	X	X	X				

(*continued*)

TOPIC AND VALUES CHART (*continued*)

EPISODE TITLE AND TOPIC	KEY DEMOCRATIC VALUES INVOLVED							
Volume 2, Part 3: Hot and Cold War (1941–1960)	Authority	Equality	Liberty	Life	Loyalty	Promise-keeping	Property	Truth
1. A Loaded Weapon *The decision of the U.S. government to relocate Japanese-Americans during World War II and the resistance of Fred Korematsu*		X	X		X		X	
2. About Face *The clash between General Joseph Stilwell and Jiang Jie-shi (Chiang Kai-shek) in China during World War II*	X					X		X
3. The Unluckiest Kid *The execution of Private Eddie Slovik*	X		X	X	X			
4. Atomic Falling-out *Robert Oppenheimer's efforts to produce an atomic bomb and the nuclear policy controversy*				X	X			X
5. Pink Lady *The 1950 U.S. Senate campaign in California between Richard Nixon and Helen Douglas*			X		X			X
6. A Clash of Symbols *Paul Robeson's achievements tempered by the consequences of his sympathy for communism*		X	X	X	X			X
7. Sky Wars *The capture by the Soviet Union in 1959 of U-2 spy plane pilot Francis Gary Powers and the response of President Eisenhower*				X				X

Volume 2, Part 4: Searching for Consensus (1961–)	Authority	Equality	Liberty	Life	Loyalty	Promise-keeping	Property	Truth
1. Rock Smites Moses *Conflict between Robert Moses and Governor Nelson Rockefeller over power and public works in New York State*	X					X		
2. What a Waste *The killing in March 1968 of villagers in My Lai, Vietnam by U.S. soldiers led by Lt. William Calley*	X			X				X
3. Fingerprince *Detective Robert Leuci's decision to expose corruption involving illegal drugs among police officers in New York City*	X				X			X
4. Cover-up Uncovered *The decision of presidential counselor, John Dean, to tell the truth about the Watergate scandal*	X				X	X		X
5. Buying Your Pardon *The exposé, by Marie Ragghianti, of the selling of pardons and clemencies by Tennessee officials*	X				X		X	X
6. Affirmative or Negative *Allan Bakke's legal challenge of the special admissions policy for disadvantaged applicants to the U. of California medical school*	X	X						
7. King to Pawn *Admission of the shah of Iran to the U.S. for medical treatment and Pres. Carter's subsequent dilemmas over U.S. hostages*	X	X	X	X	X		X	

failing to respect the privacy rights of students and their parents, for having a weak theoretical and research base, and on other grounds. The approach to treating value issues taken by this curriculum avoids these shortcomings. It recognizes that the examination of ethical value issues requires careful and serious thought. By explicitly aiming to promote higher-order thinking using values associated with democratic societies, it avoids ethical relativism—the view that all value decisions are equally defensible. The approach does not ask students to reveal personal information about themselves or their families, thereby respecting privacy rights. The theory and psychological assumptions from which the curriculum is derived have been the subject of hundreds of books, articles, and research studies. While all theory and research is, and should be, subject to criticism, the major elements of theory and the research base for this curriculum have received wide acceptance among scholars. Similarly, the rational examination of important ethical value issues has long been regarded as a vital part of citizenship education in a democracy.

Q. Even though this approach to handling value issues may not be subject to some of the criticisms leveled against other approaches, how do you respond to the claim that schools should not be involved in teaching about values, because they are a matter for the family and church?

A. There is no question that children's parents, and the religions to which they belong, do and should have an important role in the ethical education of young people. Schools also do, and should, have an important role in ethical education. One general purpose of schooling in a democracy is to prepare young people for the future—not simply for pursuing higher education or attaining particular jobs, but also for being socially responsible in a variety of roles: family member, worker, citizen, friend, etc. Individuals who are capable of analyzing ethical issues and reasoning carefully about them are more likely to recognize their personal obligations and to respect the legitimate rights of others. The curriculum is intended to help serve that goal.

There are parents who claim that if schools deal with value issues they will undermine the efforts of families and churches. This could happen if value issues were handled irresponsibly. If school programs were designed to indoctrinate students into accepting particular ethical beliefs, there would be the potential for conflict between schools and parents. The approach to ethical issues taken by this curriculum, however, rejects indoctrination. There is no secret attempt to impose a set of value conclusions on students.

The previous comments should not be taken to mean that the *Reasoning with Democratic Values* approach is neutral or noncontroversial. The authors endorse the central values of democracy while recognizing that their application to specific situations requires judgment supported by careful reasoning. There are people who will continue to object to this—people who believe that honest inquiry into some of the troublesome ethical conflicts in our history is somehow a misguided, even an immoral pursuit. To them there is little to say. The authors of the curriculum believe that schools should stand for rational inquiry and should be in the business of opening minds, not shutting them down. It is a disservice to the intellectual development of young people to pretend that ethical conflict is not an important and continuing part of history—a part worthy of study and thoughtful examination.

Q. When a classroom becomes a forum for the exchange of ideas about ethical issues, is it not likely that students will hear ideas that conflict with what they have been taught in their homes or in their churches?

A. Of course, that possibility exists. The approach taken by *Reasoning with Democratic Values* permits a variety of viewpoints to be expressed. Yet simply because a student hears an opposing point of view does not mean that he or she will reject what has been learned elsewhere. That is neither the intent of the curriculum nor its inevitable consequence. This curriculum does, however, assume that all points of view on ethical issues are subject to question. Questioning them is not equivalent to rejecting them. The practice of rational discourse does not discredit familial teachings or religious faith.

The concern expressed in the question is, at times, a legitimate one and can apply to some approaches to values education. In connection to this curriculum, however, it is an unwarranted fear reflecting a misunderstanding of the principles and practices being advocated.

Q. Do students have sufficient knowledge of history to discuss the ethical issues raised in this curriculum?

A. A substantial amount of historical background information is presented in each episode. It is recommended that episodes be used two or three times a month to enrich students' regular study of United States history. A general historical foundation can be laid before introducing a particular episode.

Q. Will the use of the *Reasoning with Democratic Values* curriculum as supplemental material in a United States history course reduce students' knowledge of historical subject matter?

A. Students do not learn less history. The content of the episodes is historical, not fictional. The episodes pursue topics in greater depth than do typical basal textbooks. For example, such events as Shays' Rebellion, the General Motors sit-down strike, or the U-2 spy plane episode receive more attention in the curriculum than they do in leading textbooks. By reading and discussing the episodes, students stand to learn more, not less, about selected topics in United States history. Related as they are to significant historical developments, the episodes may reinforce students' knowledge of major events and figures mentioned in their textbooks.

A recent study by Frances Fitzgerald charges that most United States history textbooks vapidly reduce information to the lowest common denominator. Many of the books have been sanitized in an effort to rid them of any conflict or controversy existing in the nation's history. The *Reasoning with Democratic Values* curriculum does not shy away from significant historical conflicts. It presents them as stories of the past that are engaging to students. During field tests, most students found the episodes more interesting than their textbooks. The *Reasoning with Democratic Values* curriculum promises to invigorate the study of United States history.

There is some evidence that an issues approach to United States history does not diminish students' knowledge of factual content. As a result of experiments with the Harvard Public Issues Series—similar in some ways to the *Reasoning with Democratic Values* curriculum—Donald Oliver and James Shaver report that students who studied a conventional course in United States history gained no advantage on the California American History test over students who used the Public Issues materials.

No matter how comprehensive a United States history course a teacher wishes to offer, content choices must be made. No course can include the entire scope of United States history. Inevitably, some topics must be included and others omitted. Selection of the *Reasoning with Democratic Values* curriculum as supplemental material adds depth to United States history courses with no apparent loss of breadth.

TEACHING THE EPISODES

Selecting Episodes and Determining the Frequency of Their Use

The parts that make up the curriculum follow the standard chronology of United States history. One part deals with the colonial era, another with the new nation era, and so on. Each of the seven episodes within each part presents an event characteristic of some central value theme of the era. For example, the episode "Friends and Enemies" addresses conflicts that arose over religious freedom in the early colonial period. Similarly, "A Different Drummer" addresses conflicts that arose over the Mexican War.

In selecting episodes for a course, it is recommended that the teacher first consider the units that are normally covered. For example, there may be a unit on the Puritans when topics in colonial history are being covered. If so, the unit will likely include information about religious intolerance in New England. As a result, the "Friends and Enemies" episode would fit nicely into the teacher's plans because the story of Mary Dyer is infused with the conflict between religious freedom and governmental authority.

As indicated above, the first step in selecting episodes is to connect them with themes that arise in units of study. The second step is to decide how often episodes will be used during the entire course. It is recommended that episodes be used two or three times a month to achieve maximum student interest and to help assure that the stated educational goals will be met. Although the curriculum could form the basis of an entire course, most teachers have found it more appropriately used as supplemental material.

Lengths and Formats of Lessons

Typically, either one or two class periods are spent teaching an episode. Before deciding how much time to spend teaching an episode, there are several questions for the teacher to consider:

1. How do the complexity and length of the episode match the learning abilities of the students in the class?
2. Will the episode be read in the classroom or as homework?
3. Which activities, if any, will students be assigned to do in writing?
4. Which items from the *Expressing Your Reasoning* activity will be selected for discussion in class?

Examples of the steps in both a one-period and two-period lesson plan are presented below. These examples are only two of the many possible ways that a teacher could organize a lesson based on one of the episodes in the curriculum.

A LESSON FOR ONE CLASS PERIOD

1. Students are assigned to read the episode and to write out answers to the *Historical Understanding* and *Reviewing the Facts of the Case* activities as homework.
2. Class begins with oral recitation of answers to questions from *Historical Understanding* and *Reviewing the Facts of the Case* (10 minutes).
3. Students do the *Analyzing Ethical Issues* activity at their desks, and the teacher leads the class in discussing their answers (15 minutes).

4. The teacher leads a group discussion of one item from the *Expressing Your Reasoning* activity (15 minutes).
5. The teacher guides the students in summarizing the main ideas raised during the discussion (5 minutes).

A LESSON FOR TWO CLASS PERIODS

1. Students are assigned to read the episode in the classroom and either to write out answers to the *Historical Understanding* and *Reviewing the Facts of the Case* activities or to prepare to answer them orally (30 minutes—first period).
2. Students recite answers to the *Historical Understanding* and *Reviewing the Facts of the Case* (15 minutes—first period).
3. As an entire class, in small groups or in pairs, students do the *Analyzing Ethical Issues* activity (15 minutes—second period).
4. Two items from *Expressing Your Reasoning* are introduced, one at a time, for discussion (30 minutes—second period).

However the lesson is organized, students should first read the story and respond to the questions from *Historical Understanding* and *Reviewing the Facts of the Case.* After that, the teacher must select the items to be completed. One choice to be made is whether to do both *Analyzing Ethical Issues* and *Expressing Your Reasoning* or only one of these activities. If the teacher decides to include the *Expressing Your Reasoning* activity, only some of the items should be selected because there would not be sufficient time to discuss all of them properly. For most episodes, an attempt to discuss all the items from this activity would be futile. The result would be a superficial glance at complex ethical questions, which require careful reflection and extensive dialogue.

A point to be highlighted is that teachers must make choices from among the discussion items in the *Expressing Your Reasoning* activity. The authors have ranked the items in this activity. The first item addresses the central ethical-value conflict in the episode. Subsequent items appear in order of the decreasing emphasis given to them in the episode. Although the items are presented in order of their centrality to the episode, some teachers report their most productive class discussions are stimulated by the later items.

More than two class periods could be spent teaching an episode, especially if a different format were used for each *Expressing Your Reasoning* item. Some of the formats that can be employed are: large group discussion, small group discussion, written dialogue, recorded dialogue, and historical acting. Each of these formats is described below.

Formats for Discussion

LARGE GROUP DISCUSSION: This format involves teacher-led discussion with the entire class. The purpose of this format is to enable students to compare their own positions on the selected ethical-value question with those of their classmates. During this process students discover that not all reasons are equally persuasive. The discovery enables the teacher to help students explore the characteristics of good reasons—whether offered in support of their own or opposing viewpoints.

To begin the large group discussion, the teacher asks students to make a preliminary judgment on the ethical issue. For example, the episode "Stealing North" involves a decision by a teenager, Richard Wright, to participate in an embezzling scheme while working as a ticket taker in a Jim Crow movie theater in Mississippi during the 1920s. Richard uses the embezzled funds to flee to the North to pursue his career as a writer. The teacher could select the following question: Should Richard have participated in the ticket scheme? Students would be instructed to reply, in writing, yes, no, or undecided in response to the question. Those responding either yes or no would be told to write the reasons for their choice. Undecided students would be told to write out why they are undecided about the issue.

The teacher next conducts a straw poll, by show of hands, and records the results on the chalkboard. The number of students indicating yes, no, and undecided is recorded. The teacher notes students who are undecided. They will play an active part later in the lesson.

The straw poll may show disagreement among students, that is, some indicating yes and others no. If so, the teacher asks students taking these positions to state their reasons and writes them on the chalkboard. All reasoning offered by students is subject to challenge either by the teacher or by other students. Ways of posing follow-up questions that probe students' reasoning in greater depth are presented in the next section of this manual.

The straw poll may indicate no initial disagreement among the students. All students may initially have taken the yes or no position. If so, the teacher writes on the chalkboard differing reasons offered for the unanimous position. This step enables the teacher to point out that students may agree with their classmates for quite different reasons. If there is no disagreement, the teacher may play "devil's advocate" by presenting reasons in support of the opposing point of view or may ask students to generate reasons that might be offered by someone disagreeing with them.

Whatever the results of the straw poll, the teacher writes a chart with two lists of reasons on the chalkboard. One list has reasons in support of the *yes* position; the other list has reasons in support of the *no* position. In the "Stealing North" example, the chart might look like the following:

YES, Richard should have participated in the ticket scheme.	NO, Richard should not have participated in the ticket scheme.
1. It was a chance to get even with the employers who had mistreated him in the past.	1. If Richard got caught, he would be sent to a chain gang.
2. It was his first opportunity to get enough money to flee racial discrimination in the South.	2. Richard is obligated to honor the pledge of honesty he made to the theater owner who hired him.
3. The other employees expected Richard to cooperate with them. If he didn't, someone else would.	3. Richard's family would be disappointed in him on finding out that he had stolen money.
4. Blacks weren't bound by Jim Crow Mississippi laws because they were not allowed to vote for the legislators who passed them.	4. Stealing is against the law, and Richard has a duty to obey the laws of the state in which he lives.

Once the teacher has elicited students' reasons and written them on the chalkboard, the discussion can focus on the quality of the reasons presented. The teacher can encourage students to evaluate the reasons by asking: Which is the best reason in each list? What makes it more persuasive than the others? Which is the worst reason? Why? These questions require students to reason about their reasoning.

The teacher can draw the discussion to a close by turning to the students who were initially undecided, if there were any. These students can be asked whether any of the reasoning expressed has influenced their thinking. If still undecided, they can be asked to explain the basis for their indecision.

To conclude the lesson, the teacher can highlight reasoning that seems to have had the strongest impact upon the members of the class. More details on concluding these discussions are presented in the next section of this manual.

SMALL GROUP DISCUSSION: This small group format involves groups of five to seven students in discussion of the selected *Expressing Your Reasoning* question. The purpose of the lesson is to generate a variety of viewpoints on the ethical issue under consideration.

There are two ways to group students. One is to create agreement groups by putting together students who share the same initial decision on the question. The other is to create disagreement groups, putting together students with different initial positions on the question. In both cases the teacher should begin the lesson by taking a straw poll to determine the division of opinion on the question. For example, the episode "Sky Wars" raises the question of whether President Eisenhower should have told the truth about the spying mission of U-2 pilot Francis Gary Powers.

The teacher would begin the lesson by asking how many students think that Eisenhower should have told the truth and how many think he should not have told the truth. Using the agreement group method, students with the same initial opinion would be placed together in small groups (in a class of thirty students, five or six groups should be created). Students are instructed to discuss the reasons for their initial position and to identify what they believe to be the best argument supporting their decision. This discussion usually takes from twenty to thirty minutes.

When the small group discussions are completed, the teacher reconvenes the class as a large group. Representatives from each group report to the class on the reasons their groups identified as the best for supporting their decision. The teacher can summarize the reasons on the chalkboard, listing together those that support Eisenhower's decision and those that oppose it. A large group discussion would then follow in which students would try to explain their reasoning and consider opposing points of view.

Disagreement groups, those containing students with differing initial decisions, can also be used. Students in these groups would be instructed to first explain to one another the reasons behind their initial decision. After each group member has explained his or her reasoning to the others, the groups should have a general discussion in which students try to come to an agreement on what the best response to the question would be. At the end of the small group discussion, the teacher reconvenes the class into a large group. Members of the group report on their discussion and are asked to identify the major areas of agreement and disagreement in their group.

As a variation on the above small group formats, the teacher may wish to identify students who have no initial opinion on the central question. When using the agreement group approach, undecided students would meet together to discuss the question and identify what it is about the episode that made it difficult for them to come to an initial decision. When the class reconvenes, members of the undecided group would report on the nature of their indecision. After hearing reasoning on both sides of the question from the other groups, members of the undecided group would be asked to indicate which reasons they find most persuasive and why.

When using the disagreement group approach, the teacher should place undecided students in each of the disagreement groups. Students with more definite, but opposing, initial positions would then try to persuade the undecided students to accept their point of view.

Small group lessons are most effective when students have been given clear instructions as to what should be accomplished in the group. In addition, as will be discussed later in this manual, it is also important to teach students how to carry on an intelligent discussion. Small group work has its greatest educational value when the participants understand their task and know how to carry on productive discussions.

WRITTEN DIALOGUE: In this format, pairs of students engage in written dialogue with one another. The purpose of this lesson is to help students consider systematically what constitutes careful reasoning on a selected ethical issue and to sharpen their ability to write clearly. An additional feature of the lesson is that all students, the shy as well as the outgoing, have an equal chance for active participation.

Students are instructed to write, in no more than two or three sentences, their initial decision and one major reason for the decision. For example, in "You Can't Hold Still," Peter Still, after years of slavery, manages to buy his way to freedom and move to the North. Eventually he is able to raise enough money to buy his wife and children, who had remained as slaves in the South. Later, some members of an antislavery organization, who had helped Peter raise money to buy his family, ask him to go on a speaking tour to help raise funds to buy freedom for other slaves. Peter, now in his fifties and at last reunited with his family, decides not to work for the antislavery group. One *Expressing Your Reasoning* question following the episode asks if Peter had an obligation to help the antislavery group.

In the written dialogue format, all students write their initial answer to the question and give one reason for their decision. Each student then exchanges his or her paper with another student. Students then are told to write a one- or two-sentence response challenging the point of view expressed by their partner. For example, Student A may have written:

> Peter should help the antislavery group because they helped him get his family out of slavery.

In response, Student B might write:

> Yes, they helped him, but now he's finally with his family again. Going on speaking tours would take him away from the loved ones he has a right to be with.

After writing responses, the partners exchange papers and write a one- or two-sentence response to the challenge. In this case, Student A might respond:

> His family should understand. They were slaves once and should be willing to sacrifice a little to help other slaves.

Students again exchange papers and write responses to the most recent statements of their partners. This process continues until called to a halt by the teacher, usually after four or five exchanges.

Using this format, it is useful to pair students who initially disagree on what Peter should so. By a show of hands on the initial question, the teacher can pair students quickly on initial disagreement. It is not necessary, however, for the two students of a pair to disagree. Because students must think of intelligent responses to their partners' positions, even if they agreed at the onset, the goal of developing more complex reasoning is still served.

One way to end the lesson is to have some students read aloud their written dialogues. This permits a wide variety of reasons to be aired and allows students to compare their views with those of others.

RECORDED DIALOGUE: In this format, students tape-record a modified debate. The purpose of this format is to enable students, cooperating in a small group, to construct a well-reasoned position on an ethical issue and to respond to opposing arguments presented by another group of students. The tape-recorded debate can be used to identify the characteristics of a good dialogue about an ethical issue.

After selecting an item from *Expressing Your Reasoning*, the teacher randomly assigns students to groups containing five or six members. This can be done by having students count off numbers, one through six, until every student has a number. Students then assemble with others having the same number.

Next, the teacher creates three pairs of groups, each of which will work separately in the classroom. In each pair, one group will be assigned to argue the affirmative position and the other group the negative position. If, for example, the episode being used was "Speaking His Peace," the question selected for debate might be: Should Eugene Debs have obeyed the Espionage Act? The affirmative group in each pair would argue that he should have, and the negative group would argue that disobedience was justified in this case.

To begin the debate, the teacher places a tape recorder between the groups in each pair. Both groups are then instructed to caucus for ten minutes to outline their main arguments and prepare an opening statement of no longer than one minute. At the end of ten minutes, the affirmative group sends one of its members to recite its opening statement into the tape recorder microphone. A member of the negative group then does the same. Following both opening statements, the tape recorder is stopped.

Both groups are then instructed to caucus for five minutes to prepare a response to the opposing group's opening statement. After five minutes elapse, a member of the affirmative group, one who has not yet been the speaker, has one minute to record a statement of the group's response. The same is then done by a member of the negative group. This process is repeated, five-minute caucuses followed by one-minute statements, until every member of the group has been the speaker. The concluding speaker should make a summary statement. The process will take approximately forty minutes.

The product of this process will be a tape-recorded dialogue for each pair of groups. All three of the tapes produced can be played for the entire class to evaluate. Students should be asked to look for examples of good reasoning, clear expression of ideas, and responsiveness to opposing arguments. They can also be asked to identify other strengths and weaknesses of the recorded dialogues.

HISTORICAL ACTING: In this format, students take the parts of some of the central figures in an episode and act out an imaginary, yet plausible dialogue between them. The purpose of this format is to help students better understand the points of view of the historical figures and to foster students' ability to elaborate the value issue raised by the episode.

This format can be applied effectively to those episodes in which there is a direct confrontation between the leading historical figures. For example, in "United We Sit," the story of the famed sit-down strike by auto workers in Flint, Michigan, during the mid-1930s, there is such a confrontation. In 1937, Governor Frank Murphy acted as a mediator between General Motors' executives and union leaders. Two or three students would be chosen to play the parts of the executives, two or three for the parts of union leaders, and one to play the part of Governor Murphy. The students would then be instructed to act out the negotiation. The players are instructed to try to express, as authentically as possible, the points of view of the central characters and to focus their discussions on the key value conflicts raised by the episode.

Students who are not playing the parts of the historical figures also have an important role in this lesson. The observers can be given a number of assignments. For example, some of them can be assigned to pay close attention to what the executives say and do, others to pay attention to what the union leaders say and do, and others to what Governor Murphy says and does. The observers are to note the points raised by their target characters. At the end of the enactment, the observers discuss the extent to which they believe their target characters seemed to be consistent with the parts played by the actual historical figures. In addition, the observers should indicate points where the players missed key issues. For example, the executives may have failed to mention how the strike was hurting workers in other parts of the country.

The players should also be given an opportunity to discuss what it was like trying to play their parts. The teacher may ask them, for example, what was the hardest thing about playing their parts, or how they would play their parts differently if they could do it again.

This format requires careful advance planning on the part of the teacher. For example, prior to the actual "performance," the actors should be briefed on their parts to assure that they understand some of the central points they should make. Most students cannot spontaneously portray historical figures in a realistic manner.

Conducting Discussions of Ethical Issues

DISCUSSION AS AN AIM: There is something that can be learned about ethical issues by listening to others discuss them. Silent observation of a discussion, however, will not necessarily sharpen a student's ability to participate skillfully in a discussion. By watching football games, one might learn a great deal about the game without becoming a better player. Similarly, in an English class, a student might benefit from reading the writing of others or listening to it being read aloud. These experiences alone, however, would not provide the practice necessary to become a good writer. Discussion skills, like others, require practice. One cannot silently learn to participate in rational discourse.

Oral expression in group discussion enables students to formulate their ideas more clearly. A student quietly listening to others may get the false impression that his or her own ideas are clear. When called upon to state those ideas orally, students often encounter difficulty in articulating their real meaning. The crucible of public debate tests the clarity of one's thinking.

A common roadblock to classroom discussion is the belief by a teacher that students have already mastered discussion skills. This assumption can lead to disillusionment when the teacher attempts to conduct a discussion and students lack the skills to carry it on. The temptation for the teacher may be to abandon discussion as a teaching method. An alternative, and the one recommended here, is that students be taught how to have a good discussion of an ethical issue. Since the ability does not occur automatically, it must be nurtured through patient practice. In other words, discussion skills become an explicit goal of instruction.

EFFECTIVE QUESTIONING: Questions—stimulating, thought-provoking, challenging questions—make or break class discussions. *Expressing Your Reasoning* presents focus questions for beginning a classroom discussion. Once the discussion begins, it is primarily up to the teacher to sustain it. The skillful teacher anticipates typical student responses to the opening question. Follow-up questions are then prepared to broaden students' thinking about the ethical issue involved by stimulating them to reflect upon their initial responses.

Examples of five different types of follow-up questions are presented below. They are based upon the episode entitled "Pioneer Suffragist." In that episode, Susan B. Anthony must decide whether to accept money and help from a racist who is willing to contribute to the 1867 woman suffrage campaign in Kansas. The opening question from *Expressing Your Reasoning* asks: Should Susan have accepted George Francis Train's offer of help?

Raising a Competing Value: This type of question asks a student to consider an ethical value not recognized in his or her initial comments. For example:

Student: I think Susan B. Anthony ought to accept the contribution because it is her best chance to get enough money to pay for her campaign expenses.

Teacher: How will accepting the money affect her commitment to equality?

Examining Ethical Consistency: This type of question asks a student to reconsider an apparent contradiction in what he or she has said, or to apply a position expressed to an analogous situation. For example:

Student: I think she should have refused the money, because her friends in the Equal Rights Association disapproved of Mr. Train.

Teacher: Earlier you agreed when someone suggested that we should "never look a gift horse in the mouth." How can you agree with that comment and also believe what you just said?

–or–

Student: If she intends to use the money for a good purpose, then I think it's all right for her to accept it, no matter what the source.

Teacher: Would it be right for a charity to accept funds known to be stolen?

Clarifying Terms: This type of question asks a student to make clearer the meaning of something said. Often the question asks for a working definition of a term used by a student. For example:

Student: It would be wrong for anyone to benefit from ill-gotten gains.

Teacher: What do you mean by ill-gotten gains?

Seeking Relevance: This type of question asks a student to relate a comment, the relevance of which is not apparent, to the ethical issue being discussed. It is designed to keep the discussion on track and to prevent students from straying. For example:

Student: I don't think women should have to serve in the army.

Teacher: What does that have to do with whether or not Susan B. Anthony should accept Train's offer?

Role-taking: This type of question asks a student to assume the point of view either of a different character in the story or of a hypothetical figure. For example:

Student: There is nothing wrong with her accepting help for a cause that she had been working for most of her life. This was the first time that a state might guarantee the vote for women.

Teacher: Think of this from the standpoint of Frederick Douglass, long a political ally of Susan's. What might his reaction be to her going on a speaking tour with a man who would deny the vote to blacks?

CHARACTERISTICS OF PRODUCTIVE DISCUSSIONS: A successful classroom discussion requires enthusiastic participation by students. However, simply because students are animated and vocal is no assurance that a good discussion is in progress. Discussions consistent with the goals of the *Reasoning with Democratic Values* curriculum have other features as well. Three major characteristics of a productive discussion are presented below.

Student Interaction: Students attend to the discussion by listening to each other and responding to each other's ideas. Ideally, they pose questions to one another. The discussion is not a series of interviews of students by the teacher. The flow of discussion resembles a volleyball game more than a tennis game, in that ideas are passed among students before being sent back over the net to the teacher. This pattern encourages students to challenge each other's reasoning rather than depend exclusively upon the teacher to do so. Discussion is established as a cooperative, group venture. The teacher can promote student-to-student dialogue by asking one student to paraphrase the remarks of another or by asking a student to respond to a position taken by a classmate.

Questioning: Questions of the types previously described are raised by the teacher. In addition, students are urged to pose questions to both the teacher and other students. After a question is asked, the teacher allows enough time to elapse for students to prepare thoughtful responses. The waiting time between questions helps students avoid jumping to conclusions. Questions are most effective if they trigger dissonance, that is, if they stimulate uncertainty over first thoughts and incline students to take into account important considerations previously overlooked.

Concluding Effectively: The teacher reserves some time toward the end of the period to review the course of the discussion. The discussion may come to a close with people disagreeing. If so, the teacher addresses points of disagreement and the reasons underlying them. The teacher can then ask students whether they heard any ideas they had not considered before. Another way to end the discussion is to have students draw connections between the ethical issues under discussion and contemporary events. One teacher, for example, asked students to compare the decision of the Boston police to go on strike in 1919 ("Bay State Blues") with the analogous decision by air traffic controllers in 1981. The discussion should not end abruptly. It should conclude with an effort by the teacher to summarize the major points of view that were expressed.

There are many potential obstacles to productive discussion of ethical issues. When they surface, it is best not to ignore them but to pause and point them out. Some of the more common obstacles are described below:

1. Personal Attack: Students insult other students instead of challenging their reasoning.
2. Interruption: One person begins speaking before the previous speaker is finished; more than one person speaks at the same time.
3. Dominating: One or a few students monopolize the discussion while most of the others remain silent.
4. Factual Digressions: The group quibbles at length over factual questions that divert attention from the ethical issue.
5. Personal Speculation: Members of the class predict what they *would* do if they were the main characters in the episode instead of deciding what the characters *should* have done and why.
6. Forced Consensus: The teacher presses students to reach agreement. Conflicting viewpoints are discouraged in an effort to reach closure or to inculcate a particular position.

Productive discussion is not likely to emerge immediately in classes where there has been scant experience with rational discourse. At first, obstacles to productive discussion may surface repeatedly. When group discussion becomes a legitimate aim of instruction in the mind of the teacher and sufficient time is devoted to practicing it, students will gradually improve in their ability to express clearly reasoned judgments and will become effective participants in discussions of ethical issues.

GRADING AND EVALUATION

This section presents suggestions for grading students involved in classes using the *Reasoning with Democratic Values* curriculum and for evaluating the effectiveness of programs using the curriculum. As used here, *grading* refers to the assessment of student achievement through some form of testing. The purpose of grading is to assign each student a number or letter indicating the quality of performance relative to some standard. *Evaluation* refers to the assessment of program effectiveness. The purpose of evaluation is to help teachers, administrators, and interested others to determine the educational value of a program.

Testing for Grading

Teachers seeking items for objective tests can find them in the *Student Activities* section following each episode. Questions from *Historical Understanding* address conceptual or factual meanings raised in the episode. For example, some questions deal with concepts, such as inflation, isolationism, arbitration, etc. Others raise factual questions, asking, for example, that students identify laws governing the conduct of slaves in the early 1800s, effects of the Depression, etc. Answers to these questions, as well as those in *Reviewing the Facts of the Case*, can be graded as correct or incorrect.

Activities in *Analyzing Ethical Issues* can also provide objective test items. For example, distinguishing factual from ethical issues or identifying where particular values are involved in an episode are abilities that can be graded as sufficiently or insufficiently demonstrated.

Many items in *Expressing Your Reasoning* can be used as essay questions. When using the items as essay questions, it is important that students understand that they are not going to be graded on the particular decision they make, but rather on the depth of thought they show in supporting their decision. Simply put, thoroughness of thought is what is being graded, not endorsement of any particular decision.

Prior to an essay examination, students should be told what criteria will be used in grading their answers. Among the criteria a teacher may select are: clarity of expression, consistency of logic, speaking directly to the question, and responsiveness to opposing points of view. The teacher may wish to assign a point value to each criterion. For example, on a 30 point essay question, 5 points might be alloted to clarity, 10 to consistency, 5 to speaking directly to the question, and 10 to awareness of and responsiveness to other points of view.

Of course, the grading of essay examinations, even when criteria are established, is not completely objective; of necessity, the teacher's judgment must be involved. It is possible, however, to construct objective questions that assess students' achievements of some of the reasoning goals. For example, one element of systematic thinking is the ability to identify the degree of consistency among reasons given in the discussion of an ethical issue. The following item would provide a partial measure of this ability:

> In a discussion of whether Thomas Jefferson should have freed his slaves, a student says: "Jefferson should have freed his slaves because, when writing the Declaration of Independence, he argued that a passage

condemning slavery should have been included. Even though his argument lost, he should have been true to his idea and freed his own slaves."

Which of the following statements would be most consistent with the reason presented by this student?

a. A senator should vote for a law that he personally opposes if a poll shows that a majority of the people in his state favor it.
b. People who lose arguments have no obligation to act on the views they have expressed.
c. As a general rule, people should practice what they preach.
d. It is all right for a person who says he values the right to privacy to eavesdrop occasionally on a friend's telephone calls.

In this example, statement "c" is most consistent with the student's position about Jefferson and his slaves. The creation of such items requires careful thought and is time-consuming. The example shows, however, that it is possible to design objective questions to measure some features of higher order reasoning skills.

Teachers can also grade students on their discussion skills. Many teachers try to teach their students skills of rational discussion. Some of them have developed techniques for grading student performance in discussions. In one school, teachers have developed a checklist of desirable and undesirable types of discussion behavior. Students are told that part of their grade will be based on their performance in discussions. Once or twice a semester, teachers observe small group discussions and rate the students on such criteria as: sticking to the key question, responding to the arguments presented by others, adding relevant information from the episode, etc. Students receive points for demonstrating desirable skills. Students lose points for displaying undesirable types of discussion behavior. These behaviors might include: attacking other students instead of challenging their reasoning, interrupting, dominating, making irrelevant digressions, and so forth.

Part of each student's discussion grade can be based on the quality of the group discussion, in addition to the individual's ability to demonstrate skills. A good discussion is, in part, a cooperative effort in exploring the soundness of all of the participants' points of view on an ethical issue. Therefore, part of each student's discussion grade may reflect the degree of cooperation demonstrated during the group discussion.

The above examples show how students can be graded by their teachers. The following section presents some ways that the effectiveness of the program can be evaluated.

Program Evaluation

The general goal of the *Reasoning with Democratic Values* curriculum is the promotion of social responsibility. No single measure of such an abstract goal exists. There are, however, a number of established instruments that can provide a partial assessment of progress toward the general goal.

One element of social responsibility is the ability and disposition to recognize and respect the legitimate rights of others. As mentioned earlier in this manual, researchers have found that these abilities and dispositions emerge in a developmental pattern that can be stimulated by such school practices as those advocated in this curriculum. Some measures used by these researchers are available and, when used as pre- and post-tests, enable teachers to determine whether their programs are promoting development. Two of these instruments are:

Defining Issues Test: The DIT, developed by Professor James Rest of the University of Minnesota, can be used to determine the extent to which students develop in their usage of advanced moral considerations when examining ethical issues.

Ethical Reasoning Inventory: The ERI, developed by Professor James Bode and Roger Page of Ohio State University at Lima, can be used to assess students' moral development according to Kohlberg's stages of moral reasoning.

For more information about these instruments, contact either author of *Reasoning with Democratic Values*:

DR. DAVID HARRIS
Social Studies Consultant
Oakland Schools
2100 Pontiac Lake Road
Pontiac, MI 48054
(313) 858-2004

PROFESSOR ALAN LOCKWOOD
256 Teacher Education Building
225 North Mills Street
Madison, WI 53706
(608) 263-6262

These instruments are easily administered and scored. While they provide some useful measure of program effectiveness, they should not be the sole basis of evaluation. Less formal procedures can be devised.

Students can be asked directly about their reactions to reading and discussing the episodes. Did they find the stories interesting? Did they look forward to the days when the episodes were to be discussed? Did they find the general study of United States history more interesting? Which parts of the course did they find the most stimulating, and which parts the least stimulating? Do they feel more confident in expressing themselves in discussions? Do they ever discuss episodes outside of class? What suggestions do they have for improving the quality of classroom discussion? Questions such as these can help the teacher discover students' reactions to the episodes and thus provide ideas for improving future lessons.

Teachers who are successful in teaching the episodes should be able to observe changes in student behavior over the course of a semester or two. Increases in the quality and the amount of class participation should be noticeable. Students should show an increasing propensity, when writing or speaking, for giving reasons instead of making simple assertions.

Answers for Activities

VOLUME 1

OVERVIEW

The following section includes suggested answers for the *Historical Understanding*, the *Reviewing the Facts of the Case*, and the *Analyzing Ethical Issues* activities that follow each episode in the student volumes. In addition, for each *Expressing Your Reasoning* question, ideas are presented for the teacher to use in facilitating discussion.

Historical Understanding

Following each question is an answer or answers in parentheses that would indicate that students have been able to identify the episode's larger historical context, and that they have understood some of the key concepts presented in the narrative.

Reviewing the Facts of the Case

Following each question is an answer or answers in parentheses that would indicate that students have understood some of the key details of the episode.

Analyzing Ethical Issues

This section encompasses a variety of questions and activities. (The questions and activities presented in the Instructor's Manual are usually more succinct paraphrases of the questions and activities appearing in the student volumes.) For some of the activities, the correct answers are clear (for example, identifying factual or ethical questions). For other activities, a number of answers may be correct (for example, identifying instances of value conflict). In the latter case, examples of acceptable answers are presented. Students may, of course, generate other responses that the teacher may judge to be equally acceptable. In all cases, it is important that students be able to explain the reasons for their answers.

Expressing Your Reasoning

The intelligent discussion of different points of view on these questions is central to the *Reasoning with Democratic Values* curriculum. Over time, such discussions significantly improve students' ability to express themselves, to recognize the complexity of ethical issues, and to develop carefully reasoned and well-defended positions.

One characteristic of good discussions is the presentation and evaluation of a variety of reasons in support of or in opposition to a particular ethical judgment. The discussion leader's job, in part, is to elicit the reasoning of students. Through discussion, these reasons are examined for their persuasiveness. There will be times when students express only a few reasons. The teacher may then wish to present additional reasons for the students to discuss. Thus, after each *Expressing Your Reasoning* question, some reasons are listed that the teacher may present for discussion. Sometimes the teacher will also be referred to specific pages in the student volume for additional information to use in the discussion. The listed reasons are not intended to be the best possible reasons favoring or opposing a particular position. Instead, they reflect a range of possible reasons, some of which students will reject as inadequate justifications. In the course of the discussion, students should be asked to explain why they find some reasons persuasive and others inadequate.

Volume 1, Part 1
THE COLONIAL ERA
1607-1776

FRIENDS AND ENEMIES
Mary Dyer

Historical Understanding

1. Why did the Puritans come to Massachusetts? What did they want to accomplish? (The Puritans sought religious freedom from the persecution they faced in England. They intended to establish a model society based on their religious beliefs.)
2. What did religious freedom mean to the Puritans? (Essentially it meant the freedom to practice their beliefs, as opposed to having tolerance for a wide variety of religious groups.)
3. What was the idea of the *Inward Light*? How did it conflict with Puritan belief? (The Inward Light was a Quaker belief that the will of God could be found by individuals who examined their consciences. Puritans believed that God's will could only be determined by properly qualified ministers.)

Reviewing the Facts of the Case

1. What were the provisions of the first anti-Quaker law? The second? (The first law provided for the jailing and beating of Quakers until they could be expelled from the colony. In addition, fines were imposed on those who helped Quakers. A second law provided for mutilation of Quakers who returned to Massachusetts. Still later, the death penalty was narrowly approved.)
2. How did the Puritan leaders justify the death penalty? Why did they feel it was necessary to write a justification? (It was justified as a form of self-defense, protecting the Puritan "family" from the invasion of outsiders. The leaders believed a public justification was necessary because many citizens believed the new laws were too harsh.)
3. Why did Mary and other Quakers go into Massachusetts in spite of the laws that had been passed? What happened to Mary after she received her first death sentence? (Mary and others returned to protest the laws

and to claim their rights as British citizens to travel throughout the colonies. After the first sentence, she was taken to be hanged, released, and sent back to Rhode Island.)

4. What did Captain Webb say to Mary before she died? How did she reply? (He said that she was responsible for her own death by returning after she received the warning, thereby breaking the law. She said that she was trying to get an unjust law repealed.)
5. How did King Charles react to the hanging law? (He opposed it and ordered that anyone accused under the law should be sent to England for trial.)

Analyzing Ethical Issues

Among the decisions involving the conflict of the values of authority, liberty, and life are: The decision to hang Mary, which reflected a choice of the value of authority over life; the decision to pass laws forbidding Quakers in Massachusetts, which reflected a choice of authority over liberty; the decision to release Mary after she received her first death penalty, which reflected a choice of the value of life over authority.

Expressing Your Reasoning

1. Should Mary Dyer have returned to Massachusetts? (For those students who say Dyer was wrong to return to Massachusetts, you may wish to ask them to consider: Her belief that she must follow her conscience; whether or not the law she was protesting was unjust; the claim that as a British citizen she had a right to travel freely through the colonies. For those who say she was right in returning, you may wish to have them consider: Whether or not she should have followed the wishes of her husband, or at least have discussed it with her family; whether or not she was right in knowingly jeopardizing her life; the idea that she could stay in Rhode Island and practice her religion there and let Massachusetts follow its own religious preferences.)
2. Were the Puritans right in passing anti-Quaker laws? When the Quakers kept returning, were the Puritan leaders right in passing harsher laws? (In discussing the anti-Quaker laws, you may wish to have students consider: The fact that the laws gave advance warning before the harshest punishments were imposed; the issue of whether the self-defense argument was reasonable; the extent to which a state should be allowed to direct its own affairs; the idea that the Quakers could practice their religion outside of Massachusetts; the idea that the Puritans had founded the state before the Quakers arrived.)

3. Writing assignment: Was the self-defense argument an adequate justification for the death penalty? (In discussing students' paragraphs, some of the following considerations might be raised for those who favor the self-defense argument: Should it apply when life and death issues are not at stake? For example, is a threat to one's religious beliefs, property, and so forth an adequate basis for invoking self-defense as a justification for executing someone? Those who oppose the self-defense argument might consider these points: Is there any time that the death penalty would be justified? Also, what actions, short of the death penalty, would the Puritan authorities have been justified in taking against Mary Dyer?)
4. Was Captain Webb right in saying Mary was responsible for her own death? (In discussing Webb's claim that Mary was responsible for her own death, you may wish students to consider: The fairness of the law; her foreknowledge of possible consequences of persistent law-breaking; the fact that she had once been set free after the death penalty was imposed; whether those who passed the death-penalty law were responsible; the idea that she was following her conscience.)

MADNESS IN MASSACHUSETTS
Salem Witch Trials

Historical Understanding

1. How did the Puritan settlers differ from the Jamestown settlers? (The Puritans intended to make a home in the wilderness; many Jamestown settlers were more interested in finding gold than in establishing a permanent settlement.)
2. Identify two major religious beliefs of the Puritans. (The major religious beliefs of the Puritans were striving to receive saving grace from God by becoming one of the "elect"; strict obedience to church doctrines; regular church attendance; damnation to hell for sinners; temptation by the devil to do evil.)
3. What were three difficulties faced by the early Puritan settlers? (Severe weather; problems cultivating the land; Indian attacks; disease.)

Reviewing the Facts of the Case

1. Why wouldn't Tituba talk about black magic with Rev. Parris? (The stern Puritan minister would not tolerate Tituba's beliefs, which he considered the work of the devil.)

2. For what reason might the young girls and women have become fascinated with Tituba's stories? Why did they keep their meetings secret? (Tituba's tales offered an escape from their harsh and boring lives. The meetings were kept secret because Reverend Parris would consider them sinful; attempting to speak to the dead was punishable by death.)
3. Why were the villagers relieved when the first few "witches" were named? (The accused were unpopular and not religious Puritans.)
4. What was *spectral evidence*? (Spectral evidence was alleged visions of people flying around and doing the work of the devil; since it was believed that the devil did not take the shape of an innocent person, reported visions of people doing harm were the basis for convicting them of witchcraft.)
5. Why did the girls claim that Mary Warren was a witch? (The girls accused Mary Warren because she had begun telling the truth—that the girls had been faking for sport.)
6. Why didn't John Proctor confess? (Confessing to a lie, he believed, would destroy his good name.)

Analyzing Ethical Issues

Which values were involved in each of the following decisions?

1. The judges decided to use spectral evidence at the trial. (The values of authority and truth are involved.)
2. John Proctor decided not to confess to witchcraft. (The values of life and truth are involved.)
3. Mary Warren decided not to admit publicly what she had told John Proctor. (The value of truth is involved.)

Expressing Your Reasoning

1. Should John Proctor have confessed? (In deciding whether or not Proctor ought to confess, students might consider: His pregnant wife wanted him to live; his three children depended on him; he could save his life by confessing; his family would lose his property if he confessed; he would be incriminating others by confessing to having seen them with the devil; by confessing he would be allowing the Puritan witch hunters to use him as an example; a confession would violate his commitment to truth, a basis for his self-respect.)
2. Should Mary Warren have told the truth publicly? (Considerations supporting the position that Mary Warren should have told the truth publicly include: The hoax might have ended and the lives of the accused thereby be saved; by refusing to tell the truth publicly, Mary made her

employer, John Proctor, appear to be a liar; religious authorities expected Puritans to be truthful. Considerations supporting the position that Mary should not have told the truth publicly include: She might get in trouble for starting the hoax in the first place; she would be betraying her girl friends; her friends might deny her claims and accuse her of being a witch.)

3. Writing assignment: Should the girls have privately met with Tituba? (In discussing students' paragraphs, the following considerations might be raised: Mr. Parris' disapproval; the violation of Puritan beliefs; Tituba's advocacy of black magic might be factors in arguing that the girls were wrong. The innocence of the young girls and their need for relief from the harsh New England life might be factors in arguing that the girls were right in what they did.)

HATRED ON THE FRONTIER
Whites vs. Indians

Historical Understanding

1. Identify two causes of conflict between the American colonists and various American Indian tribes. (Two causes of conflict were trickery and cheating by traders and clashes over who controlled the land.)
2. What was one underlying factor which led to tension between eastern and western colonists in Pennsylvania? (Some underlying factors include: Belief by the westerners that they were not fairly represented in the elected assembly; religious conflict between Scotch-Irish Presbyterians of the western part of the colony and Quakers in the eastern part; belief by the westerners that the colonial government did not do enough to protect them from attack during the French and Indian War.)
3. What triggered the French and Indian War? (The war was triggered by conflict among Indians, British colonists, and French settlers over the control of the Ohio River Valley.)

Reviewing the Facts of the Case

1. Why did the Paxton Boys attack the Indians at Conestoga and Lancaster? (The Paxtons believed that the Conestoga Indians had aided enemy tribes during the war, and they were outraged that the colonial assembly was protecting the Indians, one of whom was believed to be a murderer.)
2. How did the Philadelphia government respond to the attacks?

(Governor Penn offered a reward for the capture of the leaders of the Paxtons; Indians were brought to Philadelphia for protection in military barracks.)

3. What promise did Franklin and the others make to the Paxtons? (Franklin promised that the government would consider the Paxtons' requests seriously and quickly.)
4. What were the requests of the Paxtons? (They requested more military protection for the frontier, equal representation for the western counties in the assembly, and payment for Indian scalps.)

Analyzing Ethical Issues

The following are some incidents involving the identified values:

EQUALITY: Residents of eastern counties in Pennsylvania Colony had more representation in the colonial assembly than residents of western counties.

LIFE: Rewards were offered for Indian scalps.

PROPERTY: Pontiac, the Ottawa chief, attacked white settlers who were claiming frontier lands.

TRUTH: Franklin and other leaders misled the Paxtons about government intentions to consider the Paxtons' requests.

Students may propose other incidents from the story involving these four values. Those presented here are only some examples.

Expressing Your Reasoning

1. Was it right for Benjamin Franklin and the others to make promises to the Paxtons they did not intend to keep? (In deciding whether Franklin and the other leaders were right, some considerations that may be taken into account include: Misleading the Paxtons would avert bloodshed in Germantown; the Paxtons may not have been entitled to consideration of their requests because they had committed violence and were threatening more; by lying to the Paxtons, Philadelphia officials could prolong control of the colonial assembly by eastern counties; false promises by government officials might undermine trust in goverment; whatever their behavior, the Paxtons as citizens deserved fair consideration of their grievances; if they discovered the duplicity of the Philadelphia officials, the Paxtons might incite further violence elsewhere.)
2. Was it right to protect the Indians in the city? (In deciding whether or not the Pennsylvania government should have provided protection in Philadelphia for the Indians, some considerations that may be taken into account include: This group of Indians could not protect itself from the

hostile whites; Quaker religious beliefs opposed all forms of violence; the Indians were not legal citizens of the colony; bringing the Indians to Philadelphia for protection might invite an attack on the city by enraged frontiersmen; better protection was being provided for Indians than had been provided for settlers along the western frontier.)

3. Writing assignment: Should the governor have offered the reward for the scalps? (In discussing students' paragraphs, some of the following considerations might be raised for those favoring the reward: Couldn't the governor have found another way of combating enemy Indians? Wouldn't his action add to increased violence? The following considerations might be raised for those opposing the reward: His action might keep the Paxtons under control; it was one way to battle the new attacks by Pontiac's Indians; it might make up for the broken promises of the past.)

A STICKY BUSINESS
Colonial Smuggling

Historical Understanding

1. Define the following: *duty* and *mercantilism*. (A duty was a tax that had to be paid on goods brought into colonial ports. Mercantilism was an economic policy that expected the colonies to exist only for the benefit of the colonial power. As a result, trade from the colonies was restricted to its corresponding colonial power and its orbit of other colonies.)
2. Why was smuggling profitable? (Smuggling allowed traders to avoid paying the duty on their imports.)
3. Why was the British Parliament concerned about smuggling? (The government was concerned because it was losing revenue from unpaid duties.)
4. Why did the British try to enforce the Sugar Act after the French and Indian War? (They tried to enforce the Sugar Act because they wanted money from duties to help pay the costs of the war.)
5. What was *triangular trade*? (Triangular trade describes three-stop trade routes that, for example, brought West African slaves to the West Indies or southern colonies, West Indian sugar and molasses to New England, where the molasses was distilled into rum, and rum to West Africa, where it was exchanged for more slaves.)

Reviewing the Facts of the Case

1. Why did some merchants trade with the French colonies in the West Indies even though it was illegal? (It was more profitable to trade with

the French colonies. The French colonies were eager for American products and they sold their products for 25 to 40 percent less than the British island colonies.)

2. Why was the Molasses Act passed? (The Molasses Act was passed to prevent colonial trade with foreign islands by imposing a high duty on molasses imported from those islands.)
3. What were two ways shipowners could avoid paying duties? (Among the ways shipowners avoided duties were smuggling, bribing or threatening customs officials, and mislabeling cargo.)
4. What was the purpose of the Sugar Act? (The purpose of the Sugar Act was to raise money for the costs of the French and Indian War by stricter enforcement of the duty on imported molasses.)
5. What happened after the ship *Liberty* was seized by customs officials? (Dockside mobs rioted after *Liberty's* seizure, causing damage to the homes of customs officials.)
6. What happened when the British ship *Gaspee* ran aground? (A group of colonists seized the crew and burned the ship. Later they refused to tell British investigators who was responsible.)

Analyzing Ethical Issues

The following questions are either factual or ethical:

1. Could colonial merchants always make more money if they engaged in smuggling? (Factual.)
2. Was mercantilism accepted by most people during the 1700s? (Factual.)
3. Should the British have tried to enforce the Molasses Act? (Ethical.)
4. Were the British right in expecting the colonists to pay for the cost of war? (Ethical.)
5. Did colonial smuggling prolong the French and Indian War? (Factual.)
6. Was smuggling a leading cause of the American Revolution? (Factual.)

Expressing Your Reasoning

1. Were colonial traders right to engage in smuggling? (See the considerations 1.a–1.i on student text pages 31–32. Most students will be able to identify some of these reasons as more persuasive than others. They often have difficulty, however, articulating criteria that lie behind their selection of one reason over another. Establishing such criteria requires a sophisticated intellectual effort in ethical philosophy. It is unreasonable to expect students to pursue the ethical adequacy of reasons in great depth. They

can, however, be introduced to the general problem of seeking criteria for justification.

After students have identified some reasons as better than others, they should be asked to explain why they made their selections. After eliciting their explanations, you may wish to list the following ways in which reasons may be characterized:

A reason that emphasizes revenge against an offending party
A reason that stresses the self-interest of one party in the dispute
A reason that stresses the need to show compassion for one or more of the parties involved
A reason that emphasizes following custom or tradition
A reason that shows respect for legitimate authority
A reason that shows concern for the welfare of society as a whole
A reason that attempts to take into account the rights of all parties concerned

Students may be asked if any of the above characterizations fit the reasons they selected. You may then discuss whether some of these types of reasons should be preferred over others. For example: Is a reason that shows respect for the rule of law better than one that focuses on revenge?)

2. Writing assignment: Should the Rhode Island residents have told investigators who was responsible for the burning of the *Gaspee*?
(In discussing students' paragraphs, you might raise the following considerations for those who favor not telling: Weren't the British the legal authorities who must be obeyed? By not telling the authorities, residents were participating in the cover-up of a crime; the British might retaliate against the residents. For those who favor telling: Wouldn't they be getting their neighbors in trouble? Most people would not tell, to tell would go against what everyone else opposed; not telling was considered a patriotic act by those who opposed the British.)

DEFENDING THE REDCOATS
John Adams

Historical Understanding

1. What did the Writs of Assistance, the Sugar Act, the Stamp Act, and the Townshend Taxes all have in common? (They were all attempts by the British government to raise revenue by taxing the American colonists.)

2. Explain what the Sons of Liberty meant by the protest slogan "No taxation without representation." (The slogan was a protest against taxes levied on the colonists by a parliament in which they had no elected representatives.)
3. Why were British troops stationed in Boston? (Troops were sent to Boston to stem growing violence that had been triggered by new taxes.)
4. What was the Boston Massacre? (The Boston Massacre was a violent confrontation between eight British soldiers and a crowd of townspeople in Boston on March 5, 1770, resulting in the shooting deaths of five colonists.)

Reviewing the Facts of the Case

1. Identify two events that led to violence in Boston on King Street the night of March 5, 1770. (Stationing of British troops in the city; shooting of Christopher Snider by a customs official; appearance of the threatening poster near the waterfront; taunting of British soldiers by townspeople.)
2. Why was John Adams especially concerned about his family at the time of the Boston Massacre? (His wife Abigail seemed depressed and in need of his help at home; there was danger of violence against his house in the city.)
3. Why did James Forest seek out John Adams to serve as the defense lawyer for the British soldiers accused of murder? (No other lawyer would take the case, and John Adams had a reputation for being a fair and decent man.)
4. Why did Adams think this trial would draw attention in other parts of the world? (He believed the handling of the trial would be viewed as a test of the American colonists' commitment to legal justice.)

Analyzing Ethical Issues

The following questions are either factual or ethical:

1. If the British soldiers were convicted of murder, would they be pardoned by the Crown? (Factual.)
2. Should the colonies have been granted representatives in the British Parliament? (Ethical.)
3. Did Captain Preston order his troops to fire on the colonists? (Factual.)
4. Were the redcoats acting out of self-defense when they fired into the crowd? (Factual.)

5. Was it right for Boston merchants to boycott British imports after the Townshend Taxes were levied? (Ethical.)
6. Was it fair for customs officials to search homes of suspected smugglers? (Ethical.)
7. Did the Sons of Liberty think John Adams ought to defend the British soldiers? (Factual.)
8. Did the colonists have a moral obligation to pay part of the costs of the empire? (Ethical.)

Expressing Your Reasoning

1. Should John Adams have accepted the job of defending the British soldiers? (In deciding whether John Adams should have defended the British soldiers, students might consider obligations he may have had. Some possibilities include an obligation to himself, his family, his profession, the other colonists, the British government, or the principle of justice. Students could be asked which obligation, if any, was greatest, and they could be asked to state their reasons for ranking the obligations. See question 2 on student text pages 42–43, for examples of reasons supporting the position that Adams should not have taken the case. Reasons supporting the position that Adams should have taken the case include: By accepting the case he would gain favor with the Crown, the governor, and the Tories; under English tradition of law, an accused person is innocent until proven guilty and therefore entitled to a lawyer to wage a defense; due process of law would be set as a precedent in the colonies.)
2. Which would be the best reason for Adams not to take the case? (Most students will be able to identify some reasons as more persuasive than others. They often have difficulty, however, articulating criteria that lie behind their selection of one reason over another. Establishing such criteria requires a sophisticated intellectual effort in ethical philosophy. It is unreasonable to expect students to pursue the ethical adequacy of reasons in great depth. They can, however, be introduced to the general problem of seeking criteria for justification.

   After students have identified some reasons as better than others, they should be asked to explain why they made their selections. After eliciting their explanations, you may wish to list the following ways in which reasons may be characterized:

   A reason that emphasizes revenge against an offending party
   A reason that stresses the self-interest of one party in the dispute
   A reason that stresses the need to show compassion for one or more of the parties involved

A reason that emphasizes following custom or tradition
A reason that shows respect for legitimate authority
A reason that shows concern for the welfare of society as a whole
A reason that attempts to take into account the rights of all parties concerned

Students may be asked if any of the above characterizations fit the reasons they selected. You may then discuss whether some of these types of reasons should be preferred over others. For example: Is a reason that shows respect for rule of law better than one that focuses on revenge?)

3. Writing assignment: Before the trial began John Adams came to believe that the soldiers were innocent of the charge of murder. Suppose John had believed the soldiers were guilty as charged. Should he still have accepted the case? (In discussing students' paragraphs, some considerations that might be raised are: A lawyer who believes a client is guilty may not be able to provide a good defense; one should not try to help a seemingly guilty suspect avoid punishment; if accused persons are acquitted by the work of clever lawyers, the victims of crime will be unprotected; a lawyer's professional obligation is to make the best possible case, regardless of personal opinions about a prospective client; if all lawyers refuse a case because they believe an accused person is guilty as charged, the accused will be denied the right to an attorney; under the law, no one is guilty until convicted in court.)

FROM TRIUMPH TO TREASON
Benedict Arnold

Historical Understanding

1. What were three difficulties faced by the Continental Congress in preparing for the Revolution? (Among the difficulties faced by the congress were finding good military leaders, trying to establish authority over the separate states, and raising money to support the war effort.)
2. Why was control of the Hudson River important to the British? (If the British controlled the Hudson River, they could cut New England off from the other colonies and pursue a divide-and-conquer strategy.)
3. What were two reasons that made Burgoyne's surrender at Saratoga important for the colonies? (Burgoyne's surrender both prevented the British from gaining control of the Hudson River and helped persuade the French to support the American cause.)

Reviewing the Facts of the Case

1. Why was Arnold upset after the capture of Fort Ticonderoga? (He did not receive proper credit for his role in the success in a subsequent report written by friends of Ethan Allen.)
2. What hardships did Arnold face in trying to capture Quebec? (Hardships that Arnold faced included: floods, harsh weather, and disease on the trek through Maine; desertion of some of his troops; British forewarning of the attack, and the failure of needed supplies to arrive.)
3. Why didn't the Continental Congress promote Arnold in February 1777? (The congress wanted to avoid giving Connecticut too many generalships to prevent jealousy in other states.)
4. Why did many Philadelphians resent Arnold when he commanded the city? (He lived extravagantly at a time when many were coping with the scarcity caused by war.)
5. For what offense was Arnold convicted? (Arnold's offense was the use of army wagons for his own personal gain.)
6. What plans did Major André and Arnold discuss in the fall of 1780? (They discussed Arnold's plans to commit treason by helping the British take West Point.)

Analyzing Ethical Issues

Among the ethical decisions made in the story and possible reasons behind them are: Allen's friends' decision to distort the truth about Arnold's role at Fort Ticonderoga so that Allen appeared more the hero; Washington's decision to give in to Reed on the delay of the court-martial so that Pennsylvania would continue to support the war effort; Gates' decision to replace Arnold to prevent rivalry between the two.

Expressing Your Reasoning

1. How might Benedict Arnold defend his treason? What are arguments against his treason? (Arnold might defend his treason by using these arguments: He had been a hero and made sacrifices but did not receive proper recognition; his promotions were delayed; politicians were out to get him; even General Washington let him down; he had been severely wounded yet continued to be insulted; he might also claim he wanted to protect his wife from all the nasty things being said about him. Arguments against Arnold's treason might be: Treason is one of the worst of all crimes; his mistreatment was not so severe as to justify treason; as a heroic military leader, he had an obligation to stand for patriotism; he willingly

signed a loyalty oath; many people are severely wounded, insulted, and do not receive proper credit for heroics during war but do not claim that this justifies treason.)

2. Was Arnold wrong to use the army wagons for personal gain? (In discussing whether Arnold was wrong in using the army wagons, you may wish your students to consider the following: Arnold's claim that he was helping Philadelphians get supplies that they would have had difficulty obtaining in other ways because of wartime disruption; many wealthy business leaders believed in making profits during wartime; Arnold was misusing his military authority by ordering use of the wagons for personal gain; the wagons might be put to better use by supplying troops.)
3. Writing assignment: Students write paragraphs judging the rightness or wrongness of the decisions they identified in *Analyzing Ethical Issues.* (You may wish to have students read aloud their reasoning and compare it to other students who had identified a similar ethical decision.)

A LUXURY WE CAN'T AFFORD
Thomas Jefferson and Slavery

Historical Understanding

1. How did the Enlightenment influence Jefferson's view of slavery? (The Enlightenment idea of natural rights convinced Jefferson that all men, including slaves, had a right to liberty.)
2. What did Jefferson mean when he said: "We have the wolf by the ears; and we can neither hold him, nor safely let him go"? (He meant that slavery existed in the midst of American society and that either continuing it or ending it posed very difficult problems. To continue slavery perpetuated injustice; to end slavery invited rebellion.)
3. For what purpose did the First Continental Congress meet? (The First Continental Congress met in 1775 to draft a joint protest by the American colonies against recent acts of the British Parliament. The next year, the congress passed the Declaration of Independence.)
4. Why was the antislavery passage deleted from the draft of the Declaration of Independence? (The Declaration required unanimous support for passage. Delegates from some southern colonies threatened to vote against the Declaration if it contained an antislavery passage. Jefferson removed the offending passage in order to get the Declaration adopted.)
5. In what ways did some New Englanders benefit from slavery? (Some New Englanders were slave traders who operated slave ships for profit.

Others manufactured rum from molasses that was traded for African slaves.)

Reviewing the Facts of the Case

1. State two ways that slaves at Monticello were treated differently from slaves on most other plantations. (Some of the differences in the slaves' treatment were: Jefferson's slaves were better nourished and clothed; slaves were allowed to work their own gardens at Monticello; Monticello slaves were rarely lashed; when selling slaves, Jefferson tried to keep family members together, and slaves working in the naillery received extra food and clothing for their work.)
2. For what reasons did Jefferson believe that freed blacks and whites could not live peacefully together in the United States? (He believed that deep-seated prejudices by whites and the memory of injuries by blacks would produce violent uprisings.)
3. Why were Jefferson's antislavery proposals rejected by Virginia lawmakers? (The plantation economy of Virginia depended upon slave labor, and most white Virginians believed that blacks were inferior and not entitled to equal rights under the law.)
4. What economic effect would freeing his slaves have had on Jefferson? (If Jefferson had freed his slaves, he would have been deprived of the labor force upon which his income depended. Without slaves his Monticello plantation could not have functioned.)
5. What did Virginia law require of masters who wished to free their slaves? (Masters had to certify that a slave had a skill and a place of employment. It was unlawful to grant freedom without first providing for a slave's support.)

Analyzing Ethical Issues

Some places in the story where the value of equality conflicts with either the value of property or the value of authority are:

Equality versus property: Jefferson's decision not to free his own slaves because doing so would greatly reduce his income; the decision of the Virginia court not to free Samuel Howell

Equality versus authority: Jefferson's decision not to free all of his slaves because Virginia law prohibited emancipation for slaves who would be without economic support; the decision of the thirteen colonies to declare their independence from England

Students may suggest other places in the story where equality comes into conflict with another value.

Expressing Your Reasoning

1. Should Thomas Jefferson have freed his slaves? Why or why not? (Reasons in support of the position that Jefferson should have freed his slaves include: He was violating his own natural rights principle that "all men are created equal"; as a leader he had the duty to set an example; his belief in liberty was inconsistent with his behavior as a slaveowner. Reasons supporting the position that he should not have freed his slaves include: His slaves were better treated than many other slaves; he had an obligation to uphold the customs of the planter class to which he belonged; if he freed his slaves, he would go broke; freeing his slaves would probably have destroyed his political career; the time was not "ripe"—better to work gradually to change people's minds about slavery than to anger them by suddenly freeing his own slaves; the law of Virginia prohibited large scale emancipation; emancipation by Jefferson might encourage violent uprisings by slaves still in bondage.)
2. Some have argued that it might be wrong to own slaves in the twentieth century, but that during the eighteenth century it was morally acceptable. Can an action be right at one time and wrong at another? (This question raises the concept of ethical relativism—the notion that any action can be either right or wrong depending on where it takes place, when it takes place, or who is involved. Relativism can be questioned by asking students whether there are any ethical rules that should always apply. If so, what is an example of one? The Golden Rule—"Do unto others as you would have them do unto you"—could be raised for consideration. Could slavery be justified under the Golden Rule? If students claim there are no universal ethical rules, they can be asked how to judge right from wrong without them.)
3. For each situation below indicate whether you think the people involved were treated equally. (*It will be important here for students to specify a basis for comparison before judging whether or not treatment is equal.*)
   a. Virginia was allowed more representatives in Congress than Rhode Island . (If the basis for comparing citizens from the two colonies is proportional representation of population, then the two colonies were treated *equally* because the population of Virginia was greater than that of Rhode Island. If the basis for comparison is influence of a separate colony, then the treatment is *unequal* because Rhode Island had fewer delegates. This comparison can be linked to a discussion of the equality of current representation in Congress where representa-

tion in the House is based on population and representation in the Senate is the same for every state.)

b. Jefferson gave special bonuses to those slaves who produced the most nails at the Monticello naillery. (If the basis of comparison is opportunity to produce, then both groups were treated *equally*. If the basis of comparison is amount of compensation, then those who received no bonuses were treated *unequally*. Discussion of this item can include consideration of fair compensation in general. Should reward be based upon ability, effort, or productivity? Do any of these factors violate the value of equality? What determines whether compensation for work is fair?)

c. Thomas Jefferson's inheritance was greater than that of his sister. (If the basis for comparison is gender neutrality, then the daughters were treated *unequally*, because males received favoritism. This item could lead to discussion of equal treatment of offspring in matters of inheritance. Should children be treated equally in inheritance of a parent's estate? If so, what does equality require? Is it wrong for a parent to leave more property to some children than to others? The medieval European tradition of primogeniture—the legal right of the eldest child, especially the eldest son, to inherit the entire estate of his parents—could be evaluated on the basis of the value of equality.)

Short position paper: Does equal treatment of people require that they receive *identical* treatment? (In discussing students' position papers, some of the following considerations could be raised: Differences in peoples' needs; differences in peoples' efforts; differences in the value of what people produce; differences in peoples' abilities. Different treatment does not always involve inequality. For example, two people may apply for the same job, and only one is hired. Though they were treated differently, both may have been given equal consideration. Students can be asked to think of similar examples.)

Volume 1, Part 2
THE NEW NATION
1777-1850

THE DESPERATE DEBTORS
Shays' Rebellion

Historical Understanding

1. What were three reasons for the financial troubles faced by many Massachusetts citizens? (Massachusetts citizens faced financial troubles because many were in debt, were adversely affected by the West Indies trade shut down, were dependent on prices for farm goods that were not high, were required to pay taxes.)
2. Why were people throughout the United States concerned about the turmoil in Massachusetts? (The general problem of national interest was whether state government or the new central government would maintain law and order.)
3. In what ways did Thomas Jefferson and George Washington differ in their opinions about Shays' Rebellion? (Washington said government should not be overthrown but should respond to farmers if their grievances were just. Jefferson believed a little rebellion is good for government.)

Reviewing the Facts of the Case

1. What was the Court of Common Pleas? (These were courts to which debtors were taken when unable to repay their loans.)
2. What could happen to farmers who did not pay their debts? (They could have their property auctioned, their land taken, or they could be put in jail.)
3. What changes in the laws did the farmers want? (They wanted the courts to be suspended until economic times were better, paper money to be legalized, reduction in the governor's salary, and lowering of lawyers' fees.)
4. What was the Riot Act? What was the Indemnity Act? (The Riot Act permitted local sheriffs to arrest and punish rebel farmers who refused to leave an area after a warning. The Indemnity Act said rebels would not be

punished if they signed a loyalty oath and stopped trying to shut down the courts.)

5. What did Shays urge people to do in his letter to the western towns? (He urged the towns to supply men and provisions for the fight against the Massachusetts government.)

Analyzing Ethical Issues

The following questions are either factual or ethical:

1. Could Shays' men have taken control of the arsenal? (Factual.)
2. Could the Massachusetts government have afforded to make the changes the farmers wanted? (Factual.)
3. Should John Hancock have followed Sam Adams' advice about the death penalty? (Ethical.)
4. Would the rebellion have ended if Shays had followed Putnam's advice and sought a pardon? (Factual.)
5. Was it right for Shays to send the letter? (Ethical.)

Additional factual issues: Would hanging a few rebels prevent future rebellion? Would officially suspending the courts have significantly changed the farmers' economic situation? Was there widespread support for the farmers' rebellion?

Additional ethical issues: Should Hancock have granted the general pardon? Should the men at the arsenal have obeyed the order to fire on the farmers? Should the Riot Act have been passed? Were rebel farmers right in trying to shut down the courts?

Expressing Your Reasoning

1. Should Daniel Shays have sought the pardon? (Some reasons to consider for Shays to have sought the pardon are: It might have ended the bloodshed; his former commanding officer and friend had urged him to do so; it might have saved his life. Some reasons for Shays not to have sought the pardon are: The government might hang him as an example; he was fighting for a good cause and had not yet won; his followers might think him a coward.)
2. Writing assignment: Do you agree with Sam Adams that the rebellion against England was justified but the rebellion against the state of Massachusetts was not? (In discussing students' paragraphs, you may wish to have them consider: If it was right to rebel against England because of burdensome taxes, why wouldn't it be right to rebel against the state? To

what extent is the fact that the Massachusetts government was elected by the people a factor in making their rebellion unjustified? Too many people suffered from economic hard times, why should farmers act like they are the only ones? The Court of Common Pleas was established by law, so weren't the farmers required to obey it? Since the government had not responded to the farmers' efforts at getting peaceful change, what choice did they have?)

THE PRICE OF FREE SPEECH
Alien and Sedition Acts

Historical Understanding

1. What were two reasons that many Americans began to fear the French during the 1790s? (The French had had a violent revolution and there were fears that the idea of violence might spread to the United States. The French navy was attacking U.S. ships. It was believed that French secret agents were plotting a revolution in the United States.)
2. Political parties emerged during this time. What major differences existed between the Federalists and Republicans? (Federalists preferred a strong central government, pro-English policy, a manufacturing economy, and rule by the wealthy. Republicans preferred a central government with limited powers, pro-French policy, an agricultural economy, and rule by "common" people.)
3. Why did the French begin attacking U.S. shipping? (The French resented George Washington's policy of neutrality and claimed he had violated the 1778 treaty.)

Reviewing the Facts of the Case

1. What were the provisions of the Alien Acts? (The Alien Acts extended the residence requirement for citizenship from five to fourteen years. Also, the president was given power to deport any alien he regarded as dangerous to the United States.)
2. What did the Sedition Act prohibit? (The Sedition Act prohibited false or scandalous statements designed to create opposition to federal law or to bring the president or members of Congress into contempt.)
3. Why did Federalists support the Alien and Sedition laws? Why did Republicans oppose the Alien and Sedition laws? (Federalists said the

laws were necessary to protect the United States from internal conflict during a time of national emergency. Republicans opposed the laws because they claimed the First Amendment had been violated and the laws would likely only be enforced against members of their political party.)

4. What were the arguments set out in the Kentucky and Virginia Resolutions? (The Virginia and Kentucky Resolutions argued that because each state originally had to approve the Constitution, each state could decide if particular federal laws were constitutional. If a law was judged unconstitutional, it would not apply in that state.)
5. Lyon, Burk, and Baldwin all got in trouble with the law. What did each person do in violation of the law? (Congressman Lyon wrote articles claiming Adams wanted to be a king and enslave the people. Editor Burk claimed Adams lied about the threat from France and that he wanted war. In a tavern, Baldwin said he hoped a cannon salute would hit Adams in his behind.)

Analyzing Ethical Issues

The following are some incidents that involve the identified values:

Liberty: Any example of enforcement of the Sedition Act.
Equality: The law was enforced only against Republicans. Also, Lyon's claim that members of Congress should be treated differently.
Authority: Any instance in which the law was disobeyed. Also, the arguments in the Virginia and Kentucky Resolutions.
Truth: Jefferson and Madison withholding the truth that they had written the Virginia and Kentucky Resolutions.
Promise-keeping: Burk's breaking his promise to sail to Europe.

Expressing Your Reasoning

1. What are the strongest and weakest arguments against the Sedition Act? (See the arguments for consideration 1.a–1.e and 2.a–2.f on student text page 84. Most students will be able to identify some reasons as more persuasive than others. They often have difficulty, however, articulating criteria that lie behind their selection of one reason over another. Establishing such criteria requires a sophisticated intellectual effort in ethical philosophy. It is unreasonable to expect students to pursue the ethical adequacy of reasons in great depth. They can, however, be introduced to the general problem of seeking criteria for justification.

   After students have identified some reasons as better than others, they should be asked to explain why they made their selections. After eliciting their explanations, you may wish to list the following ways in which reasons may be characterized:

A reason that emphasizes revenge against an offending party
A reason that stresses the self-interest of one party in the dispute
A reason that stresses the need to show compassion for one or more of the parties involved
A reason that emphasizes following custom or tradition
A reason that shows respect for legitimate authority
A reason that shows concern for the welfare of society as a whole
A reason that attempts to take into account the rights of all parties concerned

Students may be asked if any of the above characterizations fit the reasons they selected. You may then discuss whether some of these types of reasons should be preferred over others. For example: Is a reason that shows respect for the rule of law better than one that focuses on revenge?)

3. Writing assignment: Was the tavern owner right in reporting Baldwin's remarks? Should citizens always report violations of the law? (In discussing students' paragraphs, you may wish to have students consider the following: Does it make a difference whether one likes or dislikes the lawbreaker? Does it make a difference whether the citizen would get in trouble by reporting or not reporting? Does the severity of the crime make a difference? What would happen if all citizens refused to report crimes?)

DENMARK'S GAMBLE IN SOUTH CAROLINA
Denmark Vesey

Historical Understanding

1. How did the invention of the cotton gin affect the Southern economy? (Much more cotton could be grown. The Southern economy became more dependent on the growing of cotton and on the use of slaves on plantations.)
2. Describe three of the laws that restricted slaves. (One law stated that it was illegal to teach slaves to write, another said that no more than seven slaves could travel on certain roads without being accompanied by a white

person, and a third said that slaves had to have passes from their owners when traveling alone.)

3. The Grimke sisters and some economists opposed slavery. What was the major difference between their arguments against slavery? (The Grimke sisters argued that slavery was morally wrong; economists who opposed slavery argued it was unprofitable.)
4. Why wasn't an antislavery statement included in the Declaration of Independence? (Some Southern colonies would not sign the Declaration if it specifically said slavery was wrong.)
5. How did Vesey's slave revolt bring South Carolina into conflict with the federal government? (One result of the attempted revolt was passage of the Negro Seamen's Act. The federal government claimed that South Carolina did not have the authority to make laws that violated the federal government's treaty-making powers.)

Reviewing the Facts of the Case

1. How did Denmark Vesey become a free man? (Vesey won a lottery and used some of the money to buy his freedom.)
2. Many things led to Vesey's antislavery beliefs. What were three sources of his antislavery arguments? (Three sources of his antislavery views were: the Bible, abolitionist writings, and congressional debates over Missouri.)
3. How did the authorities discover the planned revolt? (The revolt was discovered because some slaves informed white leaders.)
4. Why did Vesey call off the slave rebellion? (Knowing that authorities had been alerted, Vesey decided the revolt would be too dangerous to attempt.)

Analyzing Ethical Issues

Listed below are some of the questions raised in the story for the following values:

Authority: Should Vesey have been punished? Should the federal government object to the Negro Seamen's Act?

Liberty: Was it right to have special laws affecting slaves? Should slaveowners be allowed to prevent free blacks from visiting slaves on a plantation?

Life: Was it right to hang Vesey and the plotters? Should the revolt have been planned in the first place?

Promise-keeping: Should William Paul have told of the planned revolt?

Property: Would it have been right for Vesey to steal weapons for his planned revolt?

Truth: Should George Wilson have reported the planned revolt?

Expressing Your Reasoning

1. Do you agree with what the judge said when he lectured Vesey for having tried to organize a rebellion? (In discussing the judge's statement, you may wish to have your students consider the following: The revolt was illegal; Vesey was not a slave; many people were likely to die; slaves might suffer severe treatment after the revolt; not all slaves agreed with Vesey. What means are acceptable in overthrowing an injustice such as slavery?)
2. Writing assignment: Was it right to punish Vesey even though the revolt was cancelled and no one was hurt? (In discussing students' paragraphs, you may wish to raise the following considerations: To what extent is intent to do wrong, as opposed to actually carrying out one's intent, something to be punished? Should people be punished as a warning to others not to commit crimes? Would it be right to punish someone like Vesey to prevent the person from committing crimes in the future?)
3. Was Peter Prioleau right to inform his owners about the planned revolt? (Considerations that might support Prioleau's actions are: He wanted to avoid getting hurt; he had an obligation to his owner; many people would suffer if the revolt was not stopped; he had not agreed to remain silent. Considerations that might support Prioleau's remaining silent are: He should not turn on other slaves; no one would know he had been informed of the planned revolt; his reputation among other slaves might suffer; no harm would come to him if he remained silent.)

A WOMAN'S PLACE IS IN THE FACTORY
Lowell Mill Strikes

Historical Understanding

1. Identify two important changes that occurred in American society during the early 1800s. (Societal changes in the early 1800s included faster

and better transportation because of roads, canals, and railroads; westward expansion; immigrants adding to a growing population; and growth of a manufacturing economy.)

2. What were two reasons that textile manufacturing developed in New England? (Textile manufacturing developed in New England due to the availability of water power, an able workforce, and a concentration of capital for investment.)
3. Describe three ways that women were treated differently from men during the early 1800s. (In the early 1800s women could not vote, money earned by wives could be taken by husbands, wives did not have to be included in husbands' wills, and women were held to a stricter standard of behavior than men.)

Reviewing the Facts of the Case

1. Why were young women attracted to the Lowell factories? (Good pay, an interesting life, educational opportunities, escape from drab rural life were factors that attracted women to Lowell.)
2. Why did the Lowell system become world famous? (The factories were attractively sited and the young women workers were regarded as unusually good workers and intelligent. The magazine published by some of the workers was praised by its readers.)
3. Why was Harriet Hanson's mother fired? (She was fired because she did not prevent her daughter from going on strike.)
4. What was the *blacklist*? (A list of women who employers believed were likely to favor strikes or other forms of dissatisfaction with their employment. The list was shared by employers who would not hire workers whose names appeared on the list.)
5. Why did manufacturers' profits fall during the 1830s and 1840s? (Overproduction and an increase in the price of cotton, the manufacturers' key raw material, contributed to the fall in profit.)
6. How did the manufacturers try to keep up their profits? (Manufacturers tried to keep up their profits by cutting wages and trying to get workers to produce more goods.)
7. What was the purpose of the Female Labor Reform Association? (The association wanted to improve working conditions and to lobby for a law to reduce working hours.)
8. What reason did the state legislators give for refusing to pass the ten-hour law? (They claimed that workers took jobs of their own free will and could leave if they choose to. Also they said that workers did not need the state government to look out for their interests.)

Analyzing Ethical Issues

Among the ethical decisions made in the story are: Schouler's accusations of Cluer's immorality; the government's unwillingness to pass a law helping the workers; the labeling of women as traitors if they refused to take a pledge; the use of the blacklist; Harriet Hanson's going on strike; workers lying about illness.

Expressing Your Reasoning

1. Should the workers have feigned illness in order to stay off the blacklist? (You may wish to have your students consider the following reasons favoring the feigned claims of illness: It was the only way they could go to the convention; the employers were unreasonable in their policies; the workers believed they were fighting for a good cause; other attempts to improve conditions had failed. Reasons opposing the feigned claims include the following: It is wrong to lie; they had agreed to the conditions under which they worked and now they were breaking their agreement; they could lose their jobs.)
2. Was the *Voice of Industry* right to list the names of workers who refused to sign the pledge against working on more looms? (You may wish to have your students consider the following reasons favoring the listing: It was necessary to maintain a strong, united front; it was in the best interest of all the workers; editors of publications should be free to print their opinions. Reasons opposing the listing include the following: It was like the employer's blacklist to which the workers were opposed; people should be free to sign or not sign a pledge and not be insulted for what they decide; workers should not insult one another as a way to maintain unity.)
3. Was the legislature's opinion on freedom of contract right? (Among the issues to consider when discussing freedom of contract are: If the workers were poor and relatively powerless, in what sense did they freely agree to the contract? Should an agreement be considered "sacred" if its conditions are unreasonable? What obligations should the government have in overseeing contracts among citizens? Should company owners be free to set out whatever terms of employment they wish?)
4. Writing assignment: Should there be legal restrictions on corporations' profits? (In discussing students' paragraphs, you may wish to raise the following considerations: Should individuals be treated differently than corporations? Is it in the public interest for corporations to earn as much as they can? Does it make a difference how the money is earned? For

example, issues of monopolism, unfair competition, production of useful products, production of "fad" items, etc, could be raised.)

AN UNCONQUERED INDIAN
Osceola

Historical Understanding

1. When did the Seminole Indians first settle in Florida? (The Seminoles first migrated to Florida during the eighteenth century.)
2. What were two causes of war between the United States and Indians of the Southeast? (Two major causes of war were conflict over the return of runaway slaves and conflict over claims to the land. White slaveowners demanded that the army force Indian tribes to return runaway slaves, and white settlers wanted to settle territory occupied by Indians.)
3. To what were the inhabitants of Florida entitled according to the 1819 treaty between Spain and the United States? (According to the treaty, the inhabitants of Florida were to be "admitted to the enjoyment of all privileges, rights, and immunities of the citizens of the United States." In other words, they were entitled to the full benefits of U.S. citizenship.)
4. During the administration of President Andrew Jackson what was the policy of the United States toward Indians in the southeastern states? (The policy of the Jackson administration was to expand white settlement in the southeast and move Indians inhabiting that area to the west.)
5. How did the Treaty of Moultrie Creek differ from the Treaty of Payne's Landing? (A major difference between the two treaties was that the first, Moultrie Creek, provided the Seminoles with a reservation in Florida whereas the second, Payne's Landing, provided for movement of all Seminoles west of the Mississippi River.)

Reviewing the Facts of the Case

1. How did Osceola react to the Treaty of Moultrie Creek? (He was determined to enforce its provisions among the Seminoles, because he did not want his people forced to move west.)
2. What was Osceola's response to the Treaty of Payne's Landing? (He responded with bitterness and defiance. Rejecting the terms of the treaty, Osceola vowed to fight rather than move west.)

3. How did Osceola gain his release from the guardhouse at Fort King? (He lied to get released. His lying included an apology for his outburst in Thompson's office and a promise to accept the terms of the Payne's Landing Treaty.)
4. Why was Seminole Chief Charley Emathla killed? (He believed emigration west for the Seminoles was their best hope. Osceola and others killed him because he refused to resist removal.)
5. What were the circumstances of Osceola's capture near St. Augustine? (He was seized under a white flag of truce flying above the Seminole camp. Osceola and General Jessup were negotiating peace inside the camp when the Seminole chief was captured.)

Analyzing Ethical Issues

The following questions are either factual or ethical:

1. Were runaway slaves treated as equals by the Seminoles? (Factual.)
2. Did the United States honor the terms of its treaty with Spain? (Factual.)
3. Should the U.S. government have forced the Seminoles to return fugitive slaves to their masters? (Ethical.)
4. Were the Seminoles able to produce enough food on the Florida reservation to prevent starvation? (Factual.)
5. Should Osceola have punished Seminoles who stole food from whites outside the reservation? (Ethical.)
6. Was General Wiley Thompson right to place Osceola in irons and lock him up in the Fort King guardhouse? (Ethical.)
7. Was it fair of Seminole warriors to attack civilian plantations during the Second Seminole war? (Ethical.)
8. Why did Osceola refuse to escape from his prison cell at Fort Marion? (Factual.)

Expressing Your Reasoning

1. To gain his release from prison, Osceola lied to General Wiley Thompson by saying he agreed to emigrate west and urge his people to accept removal. Was it right for Osceola to lie? (Reasons in support of the position that Osceola was right in lying to Thompson include: Thompson was going to force the Seminoles to move west with or without their consent, and Osceola had to get released from jail to lead the resistance of his people; he had been arrested without committing a crime and was

justified in using deception to get released; lying offered his best chance to get free to take revenge against Thompson by killing him; Thompson had insulted leading Seminole chiefs and thereby forfeited his right to be told the truth. Reasons supporting the position that Osceola was wrong in lying to Thompson include: His motive for lying was to seek revenge, and vengeance is not a good motive; it was wrong to deceive the whites, just as it had been wrong for whites to make false promises to the Seminoles—if it is wrong for one group to deceive, it must also be wrong for others; by lying, Osceola was acting dishonorably, which was inconsistent with his insistence upon honor when he later declined an opportunity to escape from prison.)

2. Writing assignment: Many believed that General Jessup's capture of Osceola under a white flag of truce was an act of treachery. Jessup believed that he did the right thing. Did Jessup act rightly or wrongly? (In discussing students' paragraphs, consider how persuasively students respond to points listed in 2.a–2.f on student text pages 113–114.)
3. Since the Seminoles believed that land could not be owned in the white man's sense of personal ownership, who do you think was entitled to own the land in Florida during the 1830s? (At least three possibilities can be considered here: The land belonged to the Seminoles because they settled it first; the land belonged to the whites because they were more numerous and powerful; the land belonged to neither group and should be shared. If students take the first position, they can be asked why first settlers have a legitimate claim to the land if those who come later also need it or want it. If students take the second position, they can be asked whether "might should make right" or whether those without great power have property rights. If students take the third position, they can be asked if anyone has a right to own land, for example, the land on which a home is built or on which crops are grown. The discussion can move to broader consideration of property rights.

   What is a fair basis for determining ownership of tangible property? If students argue the Seminole position that land can't be owned, they can be asked whether the same is true for other natural resources such as water or minerals including oil, coal, or iron, and if so, why? If students argue that land can legitimately be owned, they can be asked whether the same is true for bodies of water—the oceans, for example—space, or mineral resources, and if so, why? The discussion may not produce definite conclusions, but it can raise persisting questions about fair ways to distribute land among people. By analogy to the present, students could be asked whether Indian tribes who claimed parts of the United States—including oil and gas lands—are entitled to own them today or whether Indians who claimed bodies of water hundreds of years ago should be given exclusive fishing rights today.)

4. Should Osceola have escaped from his cell at Fort Marion when he had the opportunity? (Reasons supporting Osceola's decision include: He could become a martyr—a symbol of resistance; his voluntary presence brought shame to his captors; the fight was lost and he should peaceably accept the consequences of defeat; prisoners should not escape from jail because it is against the law. Reasons supporting the position to escape include: He was captured under a flag of truce in violation of the rules of warfare and thereby not obliged to remain captive; by escaping he could continue the fight; escape offered a chance to be reunited with his family and friends; a successful escape would be a final triumph against his enemies; prisoners of war ought to try to escape.)

THE COLLAPSE OF BROTHERLY LOVE
Philadelphia Ethnic Riots

Historical Understanding

1. Identify three reasons why immigrants were often resented. (Reasons why immigrants were often resented include that their religion was often different from the majority of Americans, they were often poor, they clustered together, they worked for low wages.)
2. What position did nativists take regarding religion in the schools and the right to vote? (Nativists favored Protestant religious teaching in school and opposed any Catholic influence. They also believed laws made it too easy for immigrants to vote.)
3. In what ways did school practices offend Catholics? (Catholics were offended because they could not use their Bible in the schools and anti-Catholic textbooks were used.)
4. What were two long-term effects of the riots? (The establishment of private Catholic schools and the formation of a professional police force were two long-term effects of the riots.)

Reviewing the Facts of the Case

1. What did Bishop Kenrick request of the school board? (He asked the school board that Catholic children not be required to participate in Protestant religious activities and that they be allowed to use the Douay version of the Bible.)

2. What was the school board's response to the bishop's request? (They said Catholic students could be excused from the Protestant religious activities but could not use the Catholic Bible.)
3. How did violence first begin? (When rain disrupted a meeting of the nativists, a fight with local Irish began as the nativists ran for shelter. Exchanges of gunfire occurred.)
4. According to the grand jury, what caused the Kensington riots? (The grand jury said Catholics were responsible for the violence because of their alleged efforts to remove the Bible from schools.)
5. What did William Dunn ask of the governor? (Dunn asked the governor for permission to use guns to protect Catholic churches. The governor agreed.)

Analyzing Ethical Issues

The following are some instances involving the values of liberty, authority, equality, truth, and life:

The mob's unwillingness to obey the sheriff involved the values of authority and life.

The school board's refusal to permit Catholic Bibles involved the values of authority and liberty.

The nativists' concern about citizenship laws involved the values of liberty, authority, and equality.

The Kensington teacher's refusal to follow board policy involved the values of authority and liberty.

The nativists' effort to organize in Irish neighborhoods involved the value of liberty.

The decision to increase the powers of the militia involved the values of authority and life.

Expressing Your Reasoning

1. Should Bishop Kenrick have permitted guns to be used for defending the churches? (Among the reasons supporting Kenrick's decision might be: Guns might lead to more violence; religious leaders should not endorse violence; as the official religious leader he had authority to order whatever he chose. Among the reasons opposing his decision might be: Guns were necessary for self-defense; the anti-Irish mobs had used guns; the militia was ineffective; it was cowardly not to use guns; the governor had approved it.)

2. Writing assignment: What would have been a fair way for the school board to have treated the Bible reading issue? (In discussing students' paragraphs, you may wish to raise the following considerations: Should the First Amendment to the Constitution apply? If so, how? Protestants were in the majority, should they not have the right to control what goes on in schools? Would it have been fair to eliminate all religious activities from the schools?)

A DIFFERENT DRUMMER
Henry David Thoreau

Historical Understanding

1. What did *manifest destiny* mean to nineteenth-century Americans? (Originally the term referred to the spread of democratic government throughout the western hemisphere. It came to mean a duty or fate of the United States to expand westward.)
2. What provoked war between the United States and Mexico? (The event that triggered war between the two countries was the annexation of Texas by the United States.)
3. Why were some Northerners opposed to the Mexican War? (Northern opponents of the war with Mexico feared that slavery might be extended into territory acquired as a result of the war.)
4. What were the major provisions of the Fugitive Slave Law of 1850? (The Fugitive Slave Law of 1850 granted authority to southern slave-holders or their agents to seize and return runaway slaves found in the North. The law also prohibited citizens from aiding runaways.)

Reviewing the Facts of the Case

1. Why did Sam Staples arrest Thoreau? (Staples, the Concord tax collector, arrested Thoreau for refusal to pay his poll tax.)
2. After his release from jail, what did Thoreau reply to Emerson's question: "Why were you in there?" What do you think Thoreau meant by his reply? (Thoreau's reply to Emerson's question was: "Why were you *not* in there?" Presumably, Thoreau meant that it was right to resist the tax and that Emerson also had a duty to refuse to pay it even if that meant going to jail.)
3 How did Thoreau justify going to jail? (Thoreau claimed that refusal to pay his poll tax was a justifiable act of civil disobedience. He argued

that citizens have a duty to break laws that promote injustice. Because the poll tax supported a government that tolerated slavery, he felt obligated to refuse to pay the tax and to accept the consequences of his action.)

4. What did Thoreau do when Henry Williams arrived in Concord? (Thoreau helped the fugitive slave hide from the authorities and flee safely to Canada.)

Analyzing Ethical Issues

Places in the story where the value of authority conflicts with the value of liberty include: Thoreau's refusal of an order to use a cowhide switch on his pupils at the Concord Public Elementary School; Thoreau's refusal to pay his poll tax; Thoreau's aiding a runaway slave, Henry Williams.

If students suggest other places in the story where these two values conflict, check to determine whether liberty and authority are actually in conflict and if students can explain how the two values clash.

Expressing Your Reasoning

1. Should Thoreau have paid his poll tax? (Reasons that might be offered in support of Thoreau's refusal to pay his poll tax include: Many people avoid paying their taxes and if Thoreau could get away without paying, he should; his protest was a way to call the attention of his friends and neighbors to his opposition to slavery and the Mexican War; if people are willing as Thoreau was to pay the consequences of breaking the law, they are free to break it; Thoreau was not breaking just any law he didn't like, he was invoking civil disobedience as a principle of justice—that citizens are not obliged to comply with laws that are unjust. For reasons opposing Thoreau's decision, see 2.a–2.g on student text page 131.)
2. What do you think are the best and worst reasons for Thoreau to have paid the tax? (Refer again to 2.a–2.g on student text page 131. Most students will be able to identify some reasons as more persuasive than others. They often have difficulty, however, articulating criteria that lie behind their selection of one reason over another. Establishing such criteria requires a sophisticated intellectual effort in ethical philosophy. It is unreasonable to expect students to pursue the ethical adequacy of reasons in great depth. They can, however, be introduced to the general problem of seeking criteria for justification.

   After students have identified some reasons as better than others, they should be asked to explain why they made their selections. After eliciting their explanations, you may wish to list the following ways in which reasons may be characterized:

A reason that emphasizes revenge against the offending party
A reason that stresses the self-interest of one party in the dispute
A reason that stresses the need to show compassion for one or more of the parties involved
A reason that emphasizes custom or tradition
A reason that shows respect for legitimate authority
A reason that shows concern for the welfare of society as a whole
A reason that attempts to take into account the rights of all parties concerned

Students may be asked if any of the above characterizations fit in the reasons they selected. You may then discuss whether some of these types of reasons should be preferred over others. For example: Is a reason that shows respect for the rule of law better than one that focuses on revenge?)

3. Writing assignment: The transcendentalists believed that a conscience was the divine presence in every person. What do you think a conscience is? Is conscience the best basis for deciding what is right or wrong? (In discussing students' paragraphs, some thoughts to consider might be: Where a conscience comes from; whether a conscience changes during one's lifetime or whether it remains the same; what accounts for differences among people's consciences; whether conscience involves reasoning, feelings, neither, or both; whether a conscience can be deficient and how one ought to judge between a conscience that is adequate and one that is lacking; whether conscience guides judgment or judgment determines conscience, that is, the cause-and-effect relationship between conscience and judgment. If students maintain that conscience should not be the basis for distinguishing right from wrong, they can be asked how that distinction ought to be made.)
4. Thoreau preferred to be a vegetarian because he believed that no one should take the life of a creature that breathed. Do animals have a right to life? (Discussion could begin by comparing the value of human and nonhuman life. Students who claim that the lives of animals are equally valuable to those of humans can be asked if it is wrong to slaughter animals for food. If so, was Thoreau more ethical to be a vegetarian than a meat-eater? The consistency of reasoning by these students can also be probed by asking whether the lives of simple animals, including microorganisms and insects, are equal in value to those of humans. If so, would it be wrong to take antibiotics for an infection or to swat a mosquito? Students who claim that human life is of greater value than nonhuman life can be asked what makes human life more valuable? Possibilities include capacity for emotion, ability to communicate, intelligence, or self-consciousness. Why should these qualities, or others, be criteria for the

value of life? A corollary to the discussion can be whether humans and animals have a right to be protected from suffering. If so, why? If not, why not? The teacher can draw discussion of this item to a close by asking students to summarize their reasoning by responding to the general question: Under what conditions, if any, is it wrong to take the life of an animal? Some conditions that could be mentioned are hunting for food, hunting for sport, use of pesticides, prevention of overpopulation of a species.)

5. Should Thoreau have helped the fugitive slave, Henry Williams, escape to Canada? (Reasons supporting Thoreau's action include: The fugitive slave was desperate and needed help; to be consistent in his views, Thoreau had to oppose slavery when he had the opportunity; it was his duty to violate the Fugitive Slave Law if it promoted injustice. Reasons opposing Thoreau's action include: The danger of attack by slave-catchers; detection might bring imprisonment for Thoreau and trouble for his family; the law regarded slaves as property and prohibited aiding runaways; individuals can't make their own laws if the country is going to operate under established rules.)

Volume 1, Part 3
A HOUSE DIVIDED
1850-1876

YOU CAN'T HOLD STILL
Peter Still

Historical Understanding

1. Describe two ways in which slaves were treated like property. (Slaves were treated as property in that they could be bought and sold, they could be willed to heirs, and they could be moved wherever their owners chose.)
2. Why was it dangerous to help runaway slaves? (It was dangerous because those who helped runaway slaves risked being charged with violations of the law or physical violence from slave-catchers.)
3. Identify two ways in which the law restricted slaves. (The law restricted slaves by not allowing them to earn money without their owners' consent, not allowing them to learn to read and write without consent, and not allowing them to travel without permission.)

Reviewing the Facts of the Case

1. Why did Mr. Fisher tell the boys not to say they were stolen? (He would have trouble selling them if it were known they were stolen property.)
2. What advice did the old slave woman give to Peter? (The slave woman told Peter not to trust whites, to say what whites wanted to hear, and always to seem happy.)
3. Why did Peter's teacher demand a written pass? (The teacher could only teach those slaves who had special permission from their owners and therefore needed written proof.)
4. Why were Peter and Levin afraid of running away? (They were afraid that if they were caught, they would be severely punished.)
5. Why was Peter reluctant to marry Vina? Why did he tell his sons not to marry? (If he married Vina, he would have difficulty raising enough money to buy her out of slavery. If his sons married, it would also be difficult to buy freedom for them and their families.)

6. Why did Peter fake illness in front of Mr. Hogun? (Peter hoped that if Hogun thought he was sick that Hogun would rent him out and possibly sell him.)
7. Why did the Friedmans think the sale of Peter to himself would be illegal? (A judge would have to approve such a sale and might suspect the Friedmans were trying to get around the law.)
8. What did Kate Pickard want the Stills to do? (She wanted them to travel to meetings to support the antislavery movement.)

Analyzing Ethical Issues

What value or values were involved in the following incidents?

1. While on rental at the bookstore, Peter earned extra money at odd jobs. (Involves the values of property, authority, and liberty.)
2. Peter told his teacher that his master wanted him to go to school. (Primarily involves the value of truth.)
3. Peter told his sons not to marry. (Involves the values of authority and liberty.)
4. Peter pretended he was sick. (Involves the value of truth.)
5. Peter allowed Concklin to try to help his family escape. (Involves the values of life and liberty.)
6. The Friedmans sold Peter to himself. (Involves the values of property, authority, and liberty.)
7. When his family was freed, Peter did not help the abolitionists as they had asked. (Involves the value of liberty.)

Expressing Your Reasoning

1. Should Peter have done what Kate Pickard asked? (You may wish to have students consider the following reasons that favor Peter's helping Kate Pickard: He should return the favor because she helped him; as a former slave, he had a general obligation to do what he could to eliminate slavery; any American who opposed slavery should work against it; he had a unique experience and would be especially helpful to the abolitionist cause. Reasons not to do as Pickard asked: He had suffered enough and deserved a peaceful life with his family; he had not promised to return the favor; his life and the lives of others in his family might be endangered.)
2. Was Peter right in telling the teacher that his master, Nat Gist, wanted him to learn? (You may wish to have your students consider the following

reasons supporting what Peter told the teacher: He needed an education and that was the only way he could get it; the law restricting him was unfair; he could still do work for Gist while learning on Sunday. Reasons opposing his action: Lying is wrong; he might be punished by Gist; he was breaking the law; his master opposed what he did.)

3. Writing assignment: What would be the best argument challenging those who refused to donate money to Peter because they did not want any slaveholders to receive money? (In discussing students' paragraphs, you may wish to raise the following considerations: The money would help free at least a few people from slavery. Wouldn't giving the money at least symbolize disgust with the practice of slavery? Don't those who oppose slavery have some obligation to do something to stop it?)

FREEMEN TO THE RESCUE
Fugitive Slave Law in Wisconsin

Historical Understanding

1. What were the provisions of the Fugitive Slave Law? (Escaped slaves were to be returned to their masters by federal officials. No jury trial was needed and anyone who interfered with the process could be fined or jailed.)
2. What was the Underground Railroad? (People secretly helping slaves escape by hiding them, giving them money, and transporting them to Canada.)
3. Briefly explain the idea of states' rights. (It was the idea that states could overrule certain federal laws because each state originally had to approve the Constitution and, therefore, states had ultimate authority to judge the constitutionality of federal laws.)
4. What argument did Justice Taney give in his ruling on the Dred Scott case? (He argued that slaves were property and could not be taken from their owners without due process of law.)

Reviewing the Facts of the Case

1. Identify the following men: Garland, Glover, Turner, Booth, Paine. (Garland was a slaveowner who claimed to own Glover, a runaway slave. Turner was a free black man who supposedly led officials to Glover. Booth was a newspaper editor who led the fight against the fugitive slave law. Paine was a lawyer who originally defended Booth.)

2. Why did antislavery groups in the North oppose the Fugitive Slave Law? (They claimed the federal government was violating the principles of liberty and human rights.)
3. Why did Garland take Glover to Milwaukee? (In Milwaukee the legal procedure for returning Glover to slavery would be carried out.)
4. When Booth was arrested, with what crime was he charged? (He was charged with helping Glover escape.)
5. Why did Booth and Paine first go to the Wisconsin Supreme Court? What did the state court decide? (They wanted the court to declare the Fugitive Slave Law unconstitutional so that Booth could not be found guilty of breaking it. The court agreed.)
6. What did the United States Supreme Court decide in the Booth case? What reasons were given in its decision? (The Supreme Court said the Fugitive Slave Law was constitutional and that states did not have the authority to overrule federal laws.)

Analyzing Ethical Issues

Among the ethical decisions made in the story are: Turner's apparent turning in of Glover, Booth's calling for a protest meeting; Paine's refusal to rule against the Supreme Court decision; Taney's decision against Booth; the mob's freeing of Booth by force; Buchanan's pardon of Booth.

Expressing Your Reasoning

1. Was it right to break into the jail to rescue Glover? (You may wish to have your students consider the following reasons supporting the break-in to rescue Glover: Slavery is such an evil that the break-in was justified; the Fugitive Slave Law was unjust; there was no other way to protect Glover; a majority of Wisconsinites opposed the Fugitive Slave Law. Reasons opposing the break-in: It was against the law; they did not try other, less violent ways of freeing Glover; Glover or someone else may have been hurt or killed; those who had captured Glover were following the rules of federal law.)
2. Writing assignment: In spite of the Supreme Court ruling that the Fugitive Slave Law was constitutional, many people still helped runaway slaves to escape. Were these people wrong? (In discussing students' paragraphs, you may wish to raise the following considerations supporting those who helped runaways: Those who opposed the law were acting on their consciences and conscience must be higher than law; helping runaways was a humane act to help other humans avoid suffering; people in free states should not have to help slaveowners. Reasons opposing

helping runaways: Helping was a clear violation of the law; if they wanted to work against the law they should do so through the political system; those who helped could get themselves and their families in trouble; those who helped were depriving slaveowners of their property.)

QUOTH THE RAVEN: NO! NO! NO!
Sam Houston

Historical Understanding

1. What was the meaning of the idea *manifest destiny*? (The belief that it was right and natural that the United States should expand to the Pacific Ocean.)
2. How were United States senators elected at the time Sam Houston served in the Senate? (State legislators elected the senators for each state.)
3. How did the United States' acquisition of new territories lead to sectional arguments about slavery? (When new states were to be formed from the new territories, there was concern over whether the states would be free or slave, thus affecting the balance of slave versus free states in the Congress.)
4. What was the meaning of *popular sovereignty*? (It was the idea that voters in each state would decide whether their state would be slave or free.)

Reviewing the Facts of the Case

1. After winning independence from Mexico, it took a number of years before Texas became a state. What caused the delay? (The delay was caused by antislavery forces wanting to prevent another slave state from entering the Union.)
2. What were Sam Houston's opinions about slavery? (He did not oppose slavery and believed it necessary for the Southern economy. He feared, however, that the slavery question could lead to a civil war, which he opposed.)
3. What was John C. Calhoun's argument in favor of expanding slavery into new territories? (Calhoun said slaves were property and people should be allowed to take their property to any state they wished.)
4. Why did Sam Houston vote against the Kansas-Nebraska Act? Why were his views on the act so unpopular in the South? (He feared passage of the act would bring violence. Southerners regarded him as a traitor to the South.)

5. Why did Sam Houston work against Lincoln's election? (He believed secession would follow Lincoln's election.)

Analyzing Ethical Issues

Among other decision topics with related factual and ethical issues are:

Sam Houston's decision to vote against the Kansas-Nebraska Act.
Factual issue: Would violence have occurred if the act had passed?
Ethical issue: Was Houston obligated to vote as the majority of his constituents wanted him to?

Houston's decision to refuse the loyalty oath.
Factual issue: Would his refusal terminate his ability to lead?
Ethical issue: Should he follow his conscience?

Expressing Your Reasoning

1. Should Sam Houston have resigned as senator? (You may wish to have students consider the following reasons for supporting Sam's resignation: He should follow the majority of his constituents; he could not be effective in the Senate if others knew he was opposed by a majority of Texans; he probably would lose the next election anyway; it would be an honorable act of protest; Northerners might support him as a future president. Reasons for not resigning: It would be giving in to a wrong cause; he had a right to vote as he chose; his Senate leadership might help preserve the union; if his constituents opposed him, they could vote him out in the next election.)

2. Should Sam Houston, as governor of Texas, have taken the loyalty oath? (You may wish to have your students consider the following reasons for taking the oath: He could remain in power as governor; a majority favored it; his personal finances would remain secure; his friends favored it. Reasons against taking the oath: It was against his conscience; he would not be able to govern effectively, even if he took it; taking the oath would symbolize support of secession; he was near the end of his life and should retire.)

3. Writing assignment: Should people in each territory have the right to decide whether or not slavery would be permitted in their territory? (In discussing students' paragraphs, you may wish to raise the following considerations: The general issue of majority rule in a democracy; the question of whether some issues of human rights should not be decided by voting; the possibility that violence might break out between proslavery and antislavery forces; the general problem of when an issue should be decided on a national versus local basis.)

TEARS OF BLOOD
Robert E. Lee

Historical Understanding

1. What did South Carolina do in response to the election of Abraham Lincoln in 1860? (South Carolina seceded from the United States.)
2. How was the Constitution of the Confederate States of America different from the United States Constitution? (The Confederate Constitution emphasized the sovereignty of each state and guaranteed a right to own slaves.)
3. Prior to the Civil War, what important contribution did members of the Lee family of Virginia make to their country? (Two members of the Lee family had signed the Declaration of Independence. Light Horse Harry Lee had been a military hero of the revolutionary war and a three-term governor of Virginia.)
4. What was John Brown's goal at Harpers Ferry? (John Brown's goal was to free, by force of arms, first the slaves of Virginia and then all the other slaves in the South.)
5. What happened at Fort Sumter in the spring of 1861? (Fort Sumter, a federal fort located at the entrance to Charleston Harbor, was shelled by Confederate forces early in April and surrendered two days later to South Carolina militia units.)

Reviewing the Facts of the Case

1. As a result of his marriage, what was Lee's relationship to George Washington? (Robert E. Lee's wife, Mary Custis Lee, was the granddaughter of George Washington.)
2. What effects did the Mexican War have on the military career of Robert E. Lee? (Lee advanced his army career during the Mexican War. As an engineer, he contributed to major U.S. victories. A lieutenant at the start of the war, Lee had been promoted to lieutenant colonel by war's end. He served on the staff of commanding General Winfield Scott, who praised Lee highly.)
3. How did Superintendent Lee respond to his nephew's breaking of the rules at West Point? (Lee ordered a court-martial.)
4. How did Colonel Lee handle the capture of John Brown at Harpers Ferry? (Lee refused to bargain with John Brown, insisted upon surrender, and ordered marines to storm the building occupied by Brown and other insurgents.)

5. What was Lee's view of slavery? (Lee considered slavery a "moral and political evil" that he believed should best be ended gradually without force.)
6. What was Lee's position on states' secession from the Union? (He strongly disapproved of states' secession from the United States and believed it an unacceptable violation of the United States Constitution.)
7. What offer did General Scott make to Lee in the name of President Lincoln? (Lee was offered command of all Union forces.)

Analyzing Ethical Issues

In examining consistency between Lee's beliefs and actions, students might identify different actions than those presented below. Whatever actions they identify, students should be asked to explain the reasoning they used to determine whether or not an action was consistent with a belief. The purpose of this activity is to stimulate students to understand the concept of consistency and to begin considering the extent to which responsible individuals act consistently with their beliefs.

1. *Belief:* Slavery is a moral and political evil. (*Action:* Lee refused command of the Union Army. His action was inconsistent in that he refused to fight against slaveowners. The action was consistent, however, with Lee's belief that slavery should not be eliminated by force of arms.)
2. *Belief:* Citizens should be loyal to their country. (*Action:* Lee's resignation from the Union Army. His action was inconsistent in that an officer was expected to serve his country in wartime. The action was consistent, however, with Lee's feelings of loyalty toward other Virginians.)
3. *Belief:* The federal Union should be preserved. (*Action:* Lee's resignation from the Union Army. His action was inconsistent in that military force was required to prevent seceding states from breaking up the Union.)
4. *Belief:* One ought to provide care for sick family members. (*Action:* Lee cared for his sick mother as a boy and returned to Arlington to care for his wife. Both actions were consistent.)

Expressing Your Reasoning

1. Did Robert E. Lee do the right thing when he resigned from the U.S. Army? State the reasons for your position. (See the list of reasons in items 2.a–2.b on student text page 170.)
2. What do you think are the best and worst reasons for Lee to have resigned? to have not resigned? (See the list of reasons in items 2.a–2.b

on student text page 170. Most students will be able to identify some reasons as more persuasive than others. They often have difficulty, however, articulating criteria that lie behind their selection of one reason over another. Establishing such criteria requires a sophisticated intellectual effort in ethical philosophy. It is unreasonable to expect students to pursue the ethical adequacy of reasons in great depth. They can, however, be introduced to the general problem of seeking criteria for justification.

After students have identified some reasons as better than others, they should be asked to explain why they made their selections. After eliciting their explanations, you may wish to list the following ways in which reasons may be characterized:

A reason that emphasizes revenge against an offending party
A reason that stresses the self-interest of one party in the dispute
A reason that stresses the need to show compassion for one or more of the parties involved
A reason that emphasizes following custom or tradition
A reason that shows respect for legitimate authority
A reason that shows concern for the welfare of society as a whole
A reason that attempts to take into account the rights of all parties concerned

Students may be asked if any of the above characterizations fit the reasons they selected. You may then discuss whether some of these types of reasons should be preferred over others. For example: Is a reason that shows respect for the rule of law better than one that focuses on revenge?)

3. Should Colonel Lee have negotiated with John Brown over release of the hostages taken at Harpers Ferry? (Reasons supporting the position that Lee should have negotiated with Brown include: Brown deserved leniency or even encouragement because he was fighting against an injustice; the hostages, fearing for their lives, pleaded that force not be used against Brown; lives might be saved if Brown's deal were accepted. Reasons supporting the position that Lee should not have negotiated include: Brown's followers had already killed two men, and he should be made to pay for the killings; if Lee struck a bargain with Brown, others would be encouraged to use violence; if released, Brown would continue his violent antislavery crusade.)

4. Writing assignment: Should Lee, while superintendent at West Point, have strictly disciplined his nephew Fritz, including recommending a court-martial? (In discussing students' paragraphs, the following considerations could be taken into account: The giving of special treatment by an uncle to his nephew; the protection of one's family reputation; the duty of a superintendent to enforce discipline at West Point; the equal treatment of the accused; the benefits of lenient or harsh punishment for young people who break rules.)

THE MISERIES OF DR. MUDD
Dr. Samuel Mudd

Historical Understanding

1. Identify two ways that the Civil War made life difficult for Dr. Mudd and others in southern Maryland. (Slavery had been outlawed and farmers had to hire workers. Citizens of southern Maryland were treated harshly by Northern troops.)
2. For what purposes did John Wilkes Booth want to kidnap President Lincoln? (Booth wanted to hold Lincoln as ransom for the release of Confederate prisoners held in the North.)
3. Why did the Radical Republicans want to impeach Andrew Johnson? (They believed Johnson would not be severe in dealing with the Southern states that had fought against the North.)

Reviewing the Facts of the Case

1. Why did Jeremiah Dyer seek help from Dr. Mudd? (Dyer, Sam's brother-in-law, was being sought by federal troops.)
2. How many times had Dr. Mudd met Mr. Booth before the assassination? How did this affect him at the trial? (Mudd had actually met Booth twice, although originally he said he had met him once. Because of this, the trial judges suspected Mudd was not telling the truth.)
3. When and how did Dr. Mudd report the strangers who visited him? (Mudd reported the strangers' visit a day after they left. He told his cousin about the visit and asked the cousin to tell the federal troops.)
4. Why did Secretary Stanton want a military trial? (He believed a military trial would be faster and more likely to find the accused guilty.)
5. What were some ways that life at Fort Jefferson was dreadful? (Poor food, disease, torture, torrid heat.)
6. What did Dr. Mudd do when the epidemic hit the fort? (He volunteered his medical services to the afflicted.)
7. Why did President Johnson delay pardoning Dr. Mudd? (To pardon Mudd might make the president look pro-Southern which he feared could lead to his impeachment.)

Analyzing Ethical Issues

The following questions are either factual or ethical:

1. Did Dr. Mudd withhold information from the authorities? (Factual.)
2. Did Dr. Mudd have an obligation to treat Mr. Booth's injured leg? (Ethical.)
3. Should Mary Surratt have been treated differently from the other defendants? (Ethical.)
4. Would Dr. Mudd have been found innocent if he had been tried in a civilian court? (Factual.)
5. Was it wrong for Sam Mudd to report Henry Kelly? (Ethical.)
6. Would most of the men on the island have died if Sam had not worked so hard to save them? (Factual.)
7. Should Andrew Johnson have pardoned Sam Mudd when Frances first asked him to? (Ethical.)

Additional factual issues: Would Booth have left the burning barn? Did Sam know the injured visitor was Booth? Could Sam have successfully escaped from the prison?

Additional ethical issues: Should a civilian trial have been held for the defendants? Should Sam have hidden Dyer? Should Sam have misled the authorities regarding the number of times he met Booth?

Expressing Your Reasoning

1. Should Dr. Mudd have volunteered to help the victims of yellow fever? (You may wish your students to consider the following arguments favoring Sam's offer to help: As a doctor he had an obligation to help; he might get set free if he helped; he had experience in treating the disease. The following are some arguments against helping: Some of the victims were soldiers who had mistreated him; other prisoners asked him not to help; he might catch the disease; if his patients died, he might be accused of causing their deaths.)
2. Should Sam have revealed the name of the man who helped him in his escape attempt? (Some reasons favoring giving the name are: He might get punished if he refused; the man who helped him did not ask Sam to withhold his name if the attempt failed; the man who helped him was breaking the law. Some reasons favoring withholding the name are: He owed it to the man who tried to help him; the man would probably get punished severely; other prisoners might think him a man who could not be trusted.)

3. Writing assignment: Should Sam have hidden his brother-in-law? (In discussing students' paragraphs, you may wish to raise the following considerations: Are Sam's obligations to help a family member greater than his obligations to investigative authorities? Would it make a difference if Sam knew that Dyer was guilty of breaking some law? Were Sam's obligations to the federal authorities different because a civil war was raging?)

PIONEER SUFFRAGIST
Susan B. Anthony

Historical Understanding

1. What effect did popular sovereignty have upon the Missouri Compromise? (Popular sovereignty, provided by the Kansas-Nebraska Act, permitted new territories to allow or exclude slavery, thereby abolishing the Missouri Compromise line which had prohibited slavery in Northern territories.)
2. Why was Kansas referred to as Bleeding Kansas? (Violence erupted in Kansas between those who opposed slavery in the new territory and those who favored it.)
3. Define the following: abolitionist, freedmen, suffragist, universal suffrage, Copperhead. (An abolitionist was someone who wanted to end slavery; freedmen were former slaves; a suffragist was someone who wanted to extend voting rights, especially to women; universal suffrage is extension of voting rights to all citizens; a Copperhead was a Northerner sympathetic to the South during the Civil War.)
4. During Reconstruction, what was the major political goal of former abolitionists? (Most former abolitionists sought suffrage for freedmen during Reconstruction.)
5. Why did many Republicans and former abolitionists withhold their support for woman suffrage after the Civil War? (Many Republicans and former abolitionists believed their support for woman suffrage would lead to defeat of black suffrage.)
6. What important event occurred in 1848 at Seneca Falls, New York? (The first women's rights convention was held in Seneca Falls, New York in 1848.)
7. What were two major accomplishments of American women during the Civil War? (Outstanding accomplishments by women during the Civil War include: design by Anna Carroll of an attack plan that cut the

Confederacy in two; improvement of hospital care for wounded soldiers by Superintendent of Nurses, Dorothea Dix; and establishment of the forerunner of the American Red Cross by Clara Barton.)

8. What changes were made to the U.S. Constitution by the Fifteenth and Nineteenth Amendments? (The Fifteenth Amendment, ratified in 1868, prohibited denial of voting rights on account of race or color. The Nineteenth Amendment, ratified in 1920, prohibited denial of voting rights on account of sex.)

Reviewing the Facts of the Case

1. What two changes were proposed for the Kansas Constitution in 1867? (Two constitutional amendments were proposed, one to grant black males the right to vote and another to grant the right to vote to women.)
2. What was the Equal Rights Association and what position did it take on the issue of suffrage? (The Equal Rights Association was a group dedicated to universal suffrage.)
3. What did Miss Anthony do when Mrs. Phelps came to her in Albany for help? (She helped Mrs. Phelps and her daughter hide from the authorities.)
4. Describe the offer Susan B. Anthony received from George Francis Train. (Train offered to help in the Kansas woman suffrage campaign by organizing Democratic voters and contributing money.)
5. Why did Lucy Stone and former abolitionists dislike George Francis Train? (They considered him a racist who did not support equal rights for blacks.)

Analyzing Ethical Issues

Some places in the story where the value of equality conflicts with either the value of property or the value of authority include:

Equality versus property: Susan's decision to accept funds from Train despite his views on black suffrage—property chosen; the earnings of married women were turned over to their husbands—men's property chosen over women's equality.

Equality versus authority: Susan's decision to help Mrs. Phelps flee and hide from law enforcement officials—equality chosen; Susan's father's decision not to promote Sally Ann to the job of overseer at the cotton factory because she was female—authority of custom chosen.

Students may identify other examples where the value of equality conflicts with the values of property and authority.

Expressing Your Reasoning

1. Should Susan Anthony have accepted George Francis Train's offer of help? (Reasons supporting Susan's decision include: It is considered rude to refuse a gift; Train might be offended by rejection; Susan's best friend, Mrs. Stanton, approved; the money would be a means toward accomplishing Susan's goal of woman suffrage; after women were granted the vote, Susan could devote more energy to black suffrage. Reasons opposing Susan's decision include: Other feminists, including members of the Equal Rights Association, would be offended; Train's racist beliefs violated Susan's commitment to equality; her goals may not justify her means; by accepting Train's help, she helped further his ambition.)
2. One possible reason for accepting or rejecting each offer is presented for consideration. Other reasons presented by students and the teacher should also be discussed.
   - **a.** A slum landlord offers a contribution to build a school for nurses. (Should accept: It is a source of funds for a good cause. Should not accept: It is dishonorable to accept ill-gotten gains.)
   - **b.** A known drug dealer offers to pay college tuition for an impoverished student. (Should accept: Better for the money to go to a deserving student than for support of drug dealing. Should not accept: Acceptance of the money signifies tolerance of the criminal action.)
   - **c.** A voter is offered $25 to vote for a candidate he was already planning to vote for. (Should accept: The money has no harmful effect because it does not influence the voters's choice. Should not accept: A civic duty should be exercised without financial reward.)
   - **d.** A child is offered a pair of ice skates purchased from someone who had stolen them. (Should accept: The skates would not be returned to the rightful owner if the child refuses them. Should not accept: Receiving stolen property is a crime.)
   - **e.** A player cut from his football team offers team plays to the opposing team before the game. (Should accept: Accepting the plays improves the chances of winning the game. Should not accept: Accepting the plays would be taking unfair advantage of the opponents.)

   Some people believe the ends justify the means. Can you think of a means that would be wrong even if it accomplished a good end? (Discussion here could take into account the severity of the means to accomplish a good end. Examples of extreme means might be posed: for example, one prohibited by the Constitution—torturing a criminal suspect in order to get the names of other suspects. The discussion could also consider the broader philosophical question of whether the goodness of an end is determined by its means.)

3. Writing assignment: Those in Kansas who campaigned against woman suffrage offered five reasons to oppose the vote for women. Write a few paragraphs explaining what you think would be the best challenge to each of the arguments. (The arguments a.–e. are listed below and are also in the student book. Shown here are challenges to each argument. Consider these in discussing students' written work. In their writing, students may suggest other responses, both supporting and opposing the reasons given. Discussion could focus on whether the reasons given by opponents of women suffrage are persuasive.)

- **a.** God had given different spheres of activity to men and women. It was His wish that both remain in their appointed places. (Why were women endowed with the ability to think for themselves if it was not their place to vote?)
- **b.** Women were adequately represented by men already. (Why should women be prohibited from representing themselves? Would it be acceptable for men to be represented by women?)
- **c.** Women were unable to perform the physical duties of citizens, such as bearing arms or doing heavy labor, and thus could not defend the rights of citizenship. (Women are capable of assuming their share of civic responsibilities. Consider their contributions to the Civil War effort.)
- **d.** Women who took part in politics would neglect their household duties and destroy the harmony of home and family. (Why couldn't women balance household duties with political participation as Mrs. Stanton did and some men do?)
- **e.** Feminine purity and delicacy would be destroyed if women became active in politics. (Why should men set standards of femininity and delicacy for women? Would it be acceptable for women to set standards of masculinity and toughness for men?)

4. During the Kansas campaign, Susan's opponents argued that it would be wrong to grant the vote to women. They claimed both sexes had "different spheres of activity" and should "remain in their appointed places." For the following situations, decide whether or not you think equal consideration should be given to males and females. (For each situation, a possible reason for and against equal consideration of both sexes is presented. Discussion could focus on whether it is fair to treat the sexes differently in any of these situations.)

- **a.** Serve in military combat. (For: Those who are the strongest from either sex should be combat soldiers and the others should serve in combat support positions. Against: On the average, men are physically more powerful than women and should, therefore, do the fighting during war.)
- **b.** Do household chores such as dishwashing, laundry, cooking, or plumbing repairs. (For: Neither sex should be required to do an unfair share of unpleasant household tasks. Against: To avoid conflict, a couple should follow the traditional roles of woman as homemaker and man as breadwinner.)
- **c.** Receive time off from a job to care for a newborn infant. (For: Both parents should share in providing childcare. Against: Mothers should be near their babies, because infants are biologically attached to them.)
- **d.** Participate in high school athletics. (For: Participation in sports should be part of every student's education. Against: Sports in which one sex excels should be limited to that sex so that excellence receives maximum support.)
- **e.** Take a different last name after marriage. (For: A couple should choose whichever name they agree upon. Against: Confusion will result if the tradition of a wife assuming her husband's name is abandoned.)

THE BEAST AND THE "BAGGER"
Reconstruction in Louisiana

Historical Understanding

1. In what ways did Lincoln's plan for Reconstruction differ from the plan of the Radical Republicans? (Generally, Lincoln preferred to be more generous toward the defeated Southern states. Unlike the Radical Republicans, he was not eager to extend voting rights to blacks.)
2. What was a carpetbagger? (A Northerner who went to the South to get involved in the political and economic affairs of the defeated states.)
3. What were two causes of racial tension between blacks and whites after the Civil War? (The large number of newly freed slaves seeking employment, the issue of whether blacks should have equal political power with whites, and the social problems of equal access to public facilities.)
4. Describe three ways the federal government involved itself in Louisiana politics. (By authorizing certain governments as legitimate, by send-

ing troops to support Republican governors, by imposing loyalty oaths, and by refusing to seat elected Congressmen.)

Reviewing the Facts of the Case

1. Who was General Butler? Why was he known as the Beast? (He was the federal military commander of New Orleans and known as the Beast because of his harsh rule.)
2. Who was General Banks? What did New Orleans blacks ask of him? How did he respond? (Banks replaced Butler. Blacks requested the right to vote, but Banks turned them down.)
3. What was the Vagrant Law? Why was it passed? (The Vagrant Law was passed to control the large number of free blacks. According to the law, people without jobs could be arrested and put to work on public projects or hired out to work on plantations.)
4. Who was General Sheridan? Why was he unpopular among many Louisiana whites? (Sheridan became military commander of the district including Louisiana. He was unpopular among many white Louisianans because he refused to enforce segregation laws, and tried to allow blacks to vote.)
5. What was the Returning Board? (The Returning Board was a device created by the Radical Republicans to decide which votes should count in elections.)
6. Who was Henry Warmouth? Why did he gradually lose black and Republican support? (Warmouth was a Northerner who became governor of Louisiana. He gradually lost black and Republican support because he was not strong enough in supporting racial equality.)
7. What was the Knights of the White Camelia? Why was it created? (It was a white organization that wished to keep blacks from gaining power and equality.)

Analyzing Ethical Issues

The following are some incidents from the story involving particular values:

Authority: Butler issued the Women's Order to control the actions of disgust by some women toward federal troops.

Equality: Sheridan refused to enforce segregation laws so that the races would have equal access to public facilities.

Liberty: The Vagrant Law's passage restricted black freedom.

Life: Butler punished Mumford by taking his life.

Promise-keeping: Warmouth refused to pay a bribe that he had agreed to pay.

Expressing Your Reasoning

1. During Reconstruction, should any of the following categories of people have been denied the vote? (See student book page 206, 1.a–1.f, for the categories. In discussing this issue, you may wish to have your students identify the pros and cons of each criterion—race, literacy, property holding, and loyalty—as they might have been seen during that historical era. Students may then be asked if any of those criteria should be used today in determining who should have the right to vote.)
2. Was Warmouth right in vetoing the law that would permit blacks equal access to public facilities? (In discussing this question, you may wish to raise the following considerations: Should laws force people to be together if one group does not wish to be with another? Should it make a difference if the facility is publicly operated—for example, city-owned facilities, such as schools—or privately operated, such as rooming houses? Should the views of the majority be the deciding factor in judging whether his veto was right or wrong?)
3. Writing assignment: Would it be wrong to claim loyalty falsely to save property? (In discussing students' paragraphs, you may wish to raise the following considerations: In a democracy, should people be allowed to hold whatever views they wish? Should certain types of people be required to state their loyalty, for example, teachers, military leaders, politicians? Should the notion of innocent until proven guilty apply to the issue of loyalty oaths? Does opposition to loyalty oaths justify lying?)

Answers for Activities

VOLUME 2

OVERVIEW

The following section includes suggested answers for the *Historical Understanding*, the *Reviewing the Facts of the Case*, and the *Analyzing Ethical Issues* activities that follow each episode in the student volumes. In addition, for each *Expressing Your Reasoning* question, ideas are presented for the teacher to use in facilitating discussion.

Historical Understanding

Following each question is an answer or answers in parentheses that would indicate that students have been able to identify the episode's larger historical context, and that they have understood some of the key concepts presented in the narrative.

Reviewing the Facts of the Case

Following each question is an answer or answers in parentheses that would indicate that students have understood some of the key details of the episode.

Analyzing Ethical Issues

This section encompasses a variety of questions and activities. (The questions and activities presented in the Instructor's Manual are usually more succinct paraphrases of the questions and activities appearing in the student volumes.) For some of the activities, the correct answers are clear (for example, identifying factual or ethical questions). For other activities, a number of answers may be correct (for example, identifying instances of value conflict). In the latter case, examples of acceptable answers are presented. Students may, of course, generate other responses that the teacher may judge to be equally acceptable. In all cases, it is important that students be able to explain the reasons for their answers.

Expressing Your Reasoning

The intelligent discussion of different points of view on these questions is central to the *Reasoning with Democratic Values* curriculum. Over time, such discussions significantly improve students' ability to express themselves, to recognize the complexity of ethical issues, and to develop carefully reasoned and well-defended positions.

One characteristic of good discussions is the presentation and evaluation of a variety of reasons in support of or in opposition to a particular ethical judgment. The discussion leader's job, in part, is to elicit the reasoning of students. Through discussion, these reasons are examined for their persuasiveness. There will be times when students express only a few reasons. The teacher may then wish to present additional reasons for the students to discuss. Thus, after each *Expressing Your Reasoning* question, some reasons are listed that the teacher may present for discussion. Sometimes the teacher will also be referred to specific pages in the student volume for additional information to use in the discussion. The listed reasons are not intended to be the best possible reasons favoring or opposing a particular position. Instead, they reflect a range of possible reasons, some of which students will reject as inadequate justifications. In the course of the discussion, students should be asked to explain why they find some reasons persuasive and others inadequate.

Volume 2, Part 1
EXPANSION AND REFORM
1877-1918

RESERVATIONS NOT ACCEPTED
Chief Joseph

Historical Understanding

1. Name three tribes that whites encountered when exploring the Northwest. (Yakima, Spokan, Palouse, Nez Perce.)
2. Identify the differences between white and Nez Perce ideas about religion, property, and authority. (Nez Perce religious beliefs were related to nature; they believed that special spirits affected human and animal behavior as well as the weather. Nez Perce, unlike whites, did not believe land could be owned as personal property. The Nez Perce believed their obedience should be to traditional tribal authority; whites believed the laws of the federal government should be obeyed.)
3. Why did the United States government pursue a policy of placing American Indians on reservations? (One reason was to prevent conflict with whites who were moving onto traditional Indian lands.)
4. What were the differences between President Grant's orders of 1873 and 1875? (The 1873 order barred whites from Nez Perce lands; the 1875 order permitted whites to settle on the Nez Perce lands.)

Reviewing the Facts of the Case

1. What were the provisions of the 1855 treaty? (Large areas of land were set aside as reservations for various tribes. No whites were to be allowed on the reservations.)
2. What was the major disagreement among Nez Perce during the 1863 treaty talks? (They disagreed about whether new reservations should be established for their tribe.)
3. What did Joseph promise his dying father? (Joseph promised that he would never give up the Wallowa Valley lands.)
4. In what way did General Howard's opinion about placing the Nez Perce on reservations change from 1875 to 1877? (Initially General Howard

opposed moving the tribe to a reservation but, after some violent incidents, he came to believe that the Nez Perce should be moved.)

5. What orders did General Sherman send to General Howard as he pursued the Nez Perce? (Sherman ordered Howard to vigorously pursue the tribe to its death or turn over command to another officer.)
6. To what surrender terms did Joseph agree? Why did General Sherman and other authorities refuse to honor the surrender terms? (If Joseph surrendered, his remaining people would be allowed to return to the old reservation with their supplies. When one group of Nez Perce escaped to Canada, some authorities argued that the surrender agreement was no longer in force.)
7. What was the difference between Miles' and Howard's opinions about honoring the surrender promise? (Miles believed the surrender terms should be honored and Howard did not.)

Analyzing Ethical Issues

What values were involved in the following incidents?

1. Wahlitits' decision to seek revenge for his father's death. (Involves the value of life)
2. Howard's decision to follow orders in moving the Nez Perce onto a reservation. (Involves the values of authority and liberty)
3. Joseph's decision to surrender at Bear Paw. (Involves the value of authority)
4. The Nez Perce killing of tourists in Yellowstone Park. (Involves the value of life)
5. General Sherman's decision to oppose moving the Nez Perce to the Northwest. (Involves the values of promise-keeping, liberty, and authority.)

Expressing Your Reasoning

1. Who should have right to the land? (In discussing the issue of who should have the right to claim ownership of the land, you may wish to have students consider the following arguments: Whoever originally occupied the land has the right to have it; historically land has been claimed by those who have taken it by force, that is, the strongest have the right to ownership; whoever takes best care of the land and treats it with respect, avoiding pollution, for example, should own the land; whoever makes best use of the land for producing goods should own the land; the negotiation of treaties should decide who owns the land.)

2. Should Chief Joseph have moved to the reservation? (Reasons that Chief Joseph should not have moved to a reservation include: He promised his father he would not leave the Wallowa lands; the federal government should not take over Indian lands without their consent; it would violate his traditional spiritual views. Reasons he should have moved include: Other tribes were doing it; there might be violence if he did not move; he should recognize the authority of the federal government.)
3. Writing assignment: Should Colonel Miles have resigned? (In discussing students' paragraphs, you may wish to raise the following considerations: Miles' obligation to obey a superior officer; Miles' possible obligation to appear honorable; how his career might be affected by his decision.)

A RARE MEDIUM
Victoria Woodhull

Historical Understanding

1. Identify three social reform movements during the nineteenth century. (Women's rights, utopian communities, improving conditions for former slaves, prohibitionism.)
2. What was guaranteed by the Fifteenth Amendment? (It guaranteed the right to vote to persons of any race.)
3. How did Cornelius Vanderbilt make his fortune? (In shipping and railroads.)

Reviewing the Facts of the Case

1. What were Victoria's two general principles? (She believed there should be greater truthfulness and personal freedom in society.)
2. Victoria was the first woman to do a number of things. What were three of her firsts? (Testifying before a congressional committee, running a brokerage house, and running for president.)
3. Why were some leaders of the women's movement opposed to Victoria? (Because of her scandalous reputation.)
4. How did both Harriet Beecher Stowe and Henry Ward Beecher show their disdain for Victoria Woodhull's ideas? (Harriet Beecher Stowe, in a novel, portrayed Woodhull as a silly person; Henry Ward Beecher refused to introduce Victoria at a public meeting.)

5. What reason did Woodhull give for printing the story about Beecher? (She said her principles required that the truth be published even if injurious to a famous person.)

Analyzing Ethical Issues

The following are some incidents involving the identified values:

Delmonico's refusal to allow women into their restaurant unless accompanied by a man involved the value of equality.
Victoria's speech favoring freedoms for women involved the value of liberty.
A landlord's refusal to rent rooms to Victoria and her family involved the value of property.
Victoria's initial decision not to print the story about Reverend Beecher involved the value of truth.

Expressing Your Reasoning

1. Should Woodhull have printed the story about Henry Ward Beecher? (See arguments listed in question 2.a–2.h on student text pages 22–23.)
2. Evaluate the following arguments. (Refer again to 2.a–2.h on student text pages 22–23. Most students will be able to identify some reasons as more persuasive than others. They often have difficulty, however, articulating criteria that lie behind their selection of one reason over another. Establishing such criteria requires a sophisticated intellectual effort in ethical philosophy. It is unreasonable to expect students to pursue the ethical adequacy of reasons in great depth. They can, however, be introduced to the general problem of seeking criteria for justification.

   After students have identified some reasons as better than others, they should be asked to explain why they made their selections. After eliciting their explanations, you may wish to list the following ways in which reasons may be characterized:

   A reason that emphasizes revenge against an offending party
   A reason that stresses the self-interest of one party in the dispute
   A reason that stresses the need to show compassion for one or more of the parties involved
   A reason that emphasizes following custom or tradition
   A reason that shows respect for legitimate authority
   A reason that shows concern for the welfare of society as a whole

A reason that attempts to take into account the rights of all parties concerned

Students may be asked if any of the above characterizations fit the reasons they selected. You may then discuss whether some of these types of reasons should be preferred over others. For example: Is a reason that shows respect for the rule of law better than one that focuses on revenge?)

3. Writing assignment: Should the owners of Delmonico's restaurant have had the right to make a policy not permitting women to dine during the evening without a male escort? (In discussing students' paragraphs, you may wish to raise the following considerations: What if the restaurant had been located in a high crime area? The owner had not broken any law existing at that time. What if it had been customary for all restaurants to have such a policy? What if the restaurant's reputation would have suffered if unescorted women were allowed in during the evenings?)

THE MAINE MAGNETIC MAN
James G. Blaine

Historical Understanding

1. Identify one economic, social, and political characteristic of the United States during the period 1865–1885. (Rapid industrial growth and expansion of railroads; increasing numbers of immigrants; internal divisions in the Republican party.)
2. Why was the Republican party expecting difficulty in winning the election of 1876? (Grant's Republican administration had been tainted with scandals and the Republicans did not have a popular candidate with a reputation for honesty.)
3. Why did the presence of Chinese immigrants in California lead to tensions during the 1870s? (The immigrants often worked for lower wages than native-born workers, and their manners and customs often seemed strange to those unfamiliar with them.)
4. Identify three competing groups in the Republican party in 1880. How did the groups differ from one another? (The Stalwarts wanted Grant to run for a third term; the Mugwumps called for reforms such as civil service instead of patronage; the Half-Breeds opposed Grant and wanted Blaine to run for president.)

Reviewing the Facts of the Case

1. Why was James G. Blaine called "the magnetic man"? (Because his personality was so attractive.)
2. Who was Roscoe Conkling? Why did he and Blaine become enemies? (Conkling was a powerful New York Republican leader. He and Blaine had different personalities and clashed initially over an attempt to create a permanent military bureau.)
3. What were the Mulligan letters? How did they affect Blaine's political career? (They were letters that Blaine had written to a railroad executive. The letters allegedly showed that Blaine had been involved in shady dealings.)
4. What was Blaine's opinion about Chinese immigration? (He wanted to end Chinese immigration because he believed such a move would help restore order in California and would help get unemployed whites back to work.)
5. It is believed Garfield made a promise to Conkling. What was the promise? (Garfield allegedly offered Conkling control of patronage in New York in exchange for his political support.)

Analyzing Ethical Issues

The following questions are either factual or ethical:

1. Should James G. Blaine have fought with the Union Army? (Ethical.)
2. Was Blaine wrong in helping the railroad? (Ethical.)
3. Did the Mulligan letters prove Blaine had done something wrong? (Factual.)
4. Did the Mulligan letters keep Blaine from winning the presidency? (Factual.)
5. What caused Blaine to faint in 1876? (Factual.)
6. Would passage of the Chinese Exclusion Act have restored law and order in California? (Factual.)
7. Was it wrong for Conkling to refuse to help Blaine in the 1884 election? (Ethical.)
8. Should Garfield have rewarded Conkling for his help in the 1880 election? (Ethical.)

Expressing Your Reasoning

1. Was Blaine justified in refusing to return or make public the Mulligan letters? (In discussing this question, you may wish to have students

consider the following possible reasons supporting Blaine's action: The letters were Blaine's private correspondence, and Mulligan was hoping to use the letters just to defame Blaine; the businessman to whom he had written would probably have not approved of the publicity. Possible reasons for publicizing the letters: As a major political leader, Blaine had a public obligation to show if he was honest or not; by withholding the letters he might be withholding evidence of a crime and preventing law authorities from doing their job; by withholding the letters he made it appear he was guilty of wrongdoing.)

2. Should Chinese immigration have been stopped in the 1870s? (Possible reasons favoring an end to immigration: It might stop violence; it would provide more jobs for U.S. citizens. Possible reasons for continuing immigration: There was a treaty with China; it would be racial discrimination; cheap labor was needed for industrial development.)
3. Writing assignment: Should Blaine have joined the Union Army? (In discussing students' paragraphs, you may wish to raise the following considerations: Hiring substitutes was legal; only people with money could avoid military service; Blaine could help the North in other ways; he had urged others to join.)

A SIMPLE ACT OF JUSTICE
John Peter Altgeld

Historical Understanding

1. Who were the *Know-Nothings*? (They were a secret political organization opposed to immigrants, especially those of the Catholic faith.)
2. After the Civil War, what were two factors that attracted easterners to the West? (There was free land under the provisions of the Homestead Act and railroad construction offered well-paying jobs.)
3. Briefly describe the Granger movement. (It was a political movement of farmers who suffered from bad financial times and were determined to elect officials who would help them.)
4. What kind of a city was Chicago during the late nineteenth century? (It was a rapidly growing industrial city with a large immigrant population, often the scene of conflict between labor and industry.)
5. Briefly describe the relationship between employers and Chicago's early labor unions. (Employers generally refused to recognize the unions as legitimate representatives of the workers.)

6. What kind of society did the anarchists seek? (They sought a society without laws and government.)

Reviewing the Facts of the Case

1. How did Altgeld pay back the neighboring farmer who bought him a new suit and overcoat? (He secretly gave the farmer wheat from his father's barn.)
2. Why did Altgeld leave Ohio? (His girlfriend's family rejected him, he did not get along with his father, and he was bored by small town life.)
3. What were three reforms Governor Altgeld planned for Illinois? (Among the reforms he planned were changes in labor law, prison conditions, and public education.)
4. What happened at Haymarket Square? (An anarchist meeting was being broken up by police, and a bomb was thrown that killed seven police officers.)
5. What sentence was handed down by the judge in the Haymarket trial? (Eight anarchists were found guilty of murder. The judge sentenced seven of them to death and one of them to a fifteen-year prison term. Two of those receiving a death sentence begged for mercy and had their sentences reduced to life imprisonment.)
6. What were Altgeld's reasons for pardoning the anarchists? (He was convinced the anarchists were not guilty of murder and that they had not received a fair trial because the judge and jury had been prejudiced against them.)

Analyzing Ethical Issues

Some arguments made about punishing those convicted of murder at Haymarket Square are presented below. Decide which purpose for punishment is implied in each argument.

1. The right to life of the policemen killed was not respected by the murderers. Now they must forfeit their own lives. (Retribution.)
2. Whether these anarchists are guilty or not, hanging them will restore calm in our city between employers and workers. (Deterrence.)
3. Executing these men is unnecessary. By putting them in prison for life we will be safe from their violent deeds. (Disablement.)
4. Those who try to destroy the American way of life should not be allowed to enjoy it. Hang the revolutionaries. (Retribution.)
5. Send the anarchists back where they came from. It is the only way to protect our society from their alien ideas. (Disablement.)

6. What they need is education about democracy. If they were taught how our Constitution and laws work, they would learn respect for government authority. While in jail they must discover the errors of their ways. (Rehabilitation.)

Expressing Your Reasoning

1. Should Governor Altgeld have granted a pardon to the three imprisoned anarchists? (For some reasons against granting of the pardon, see items 2.a–2.e on student text page 46. Some reasons supporting Altgeld's decision to pardon the anarchists are: It pleased his good friend, Clarence Darrow; it showed mercy for the condemned men; the governor was exercising his legal authority to pardon convicts; without his pardon, Altgeld believed innocent men would lose their lives; no one should be punished without a fair trial.)
2. The governor's critics offered reasons against the granting of a pardon by Altgeld. Which do you think is the best reason? Which is the worst? Explain your basis for evaluating these reasons. (Refer again to 2.a–2.e on student text page 46. Most students will be able to identify some reasons as more persuasive than others. They often have difficulty, however, articulating criteria that lie behind their selection of one reason over another. Establishing such criteria requires a sophisticated intellectual effort in ethical philosophy. It is unreasonable to expect students to pursue the ethical adequacy of reasons in great depth. They can, however, be introduced to the general problem of seeking criteria for justification.)

    After students have identified some reasons as better than others, they should be asked to explain why they made their selections. After eliciting their explanations, you may wish to present the following ways in which reasons may be characterized:

    A reason that emphasizes revenge against an offending party
    A reason that stresses the self-interest of one party in the dispute
    A reason that focuses on showing compassion for one or more of the parties involved
    A reason that emphasizes following custom or tradition
    A reason that underscores respect for maintaining legal authority
    A reason that shows concern for the welfare of society as a whole
    A reason that attempts to take into account the rights of all parties concerned

Students may be asked if any of the above characterizations fit the reasons they selected. You may then discuss whether some of these types of reasons should be preferred over others. For example: Is a reason that shows respect for the rule of law better than one that focuses on revenge?)

3. Writing assignment: Some claim the Haymarket anarchists were punished for their beliefs and not their actions. Could it ever be right to punish someone for his or her beliefs? (In discussing students' written positions, you may wish to pose some of the following questions: Should expression of extreme beliefs be tolerated under the law, for example, beliefs in violence, treason, or defamation? Why was the First Amendment designed to protect the expression of unpopular beliefs? How might government attempts to control citizens' beliefs affect democracy?)

THRONE OVERTHROWN
Hawaiian Revolution

Historical Understanding

1. Describe one social, one economic, and one political effect of foreign influence in Hawaii. (Epidemics of disease occurred, schools and a formal written Hawaiian language were established; new mechanical and agricultural skills were taught, and Hawaii became a trading center; formal laws and a constitution were established.)
2. In addition to its natural beauty, why was Hawaii attractive to foreign nations? (It was a natural place for ships to obtain supplies; also sugar plantations could be established.)
3. How did the United States' tariffs affect the Hawaiian economy? (U.S. tariffs restricted Hawaiian trade in the United States and hurt the Hawaiian economy.)
4. Why did many Americans believe the United States had a special interest in Hawaii? (U.S. missionaries had done much to affect Hawaii, and Hawaii was seen as strategically important to protect the West Coast.)

Reviewing the Facts of the Case

1. What was the Hawaiian League? Why did its members oppose King Kalakaua? (The League was a semisecret organization of planters and business leaders. They opposed the king because they believed that he was corrupt, that he had created large debts, and that he had kept business leaders from power.)
2. What was the Bayonet Constitution? (It was a new constitution that reduced the king's powers, which had been forced on him by threat of force.)

3. What were the provisions of the 1875 reciprocity treaty? (It permitted Hawaiian goods to be sold in the United States without a tariff. In exchange, U.S. goods could be sold in Hawaii without a tariff.)
4. What was the Annexation Club? Why did its members oppose Queen Liliuokalani? (The club was a secret organization of business leaders who sought annexation to the United States. They believed that the queen was seeking to extend her power, and they objected to her policies on gambling and opium.)
5. Who was John Stevens? (Stevens was the U.S. foreign minister to Hawaii in 1893.)
6. What did James Blount conclude as a result of his investigation? (Blount concluded that the revolution would not have succeeded without the involvement of U.S. troops and that most Hawaiians opposed the revolution.)
7. What reason did Sanford Dole give for refusing to yield the authority of the provisional government to the queen? (His main argument was that the United States had recognized the legitimacy of the provisional government.)

Analyzing Ethical Issues

The following questions are either factual or ethical:

1. Did native Hawaiians benefit from the existence of sugar plantations? (Factual.)
2. Should Walter Gibson have been allowed to hold more than one government office? (Ethical.)
3. Was Sanford Dole right in accepting the leadership of the provisional government? (Ethical.)
4. Would the Hawaiian revolution have succeeded without the landing of U.S. troops? (Factual.)
5. Should Queen Liliuokalani have taken an oath to support the 1887 constitution? (Ethical.)
6. Would passage of a lottery bill have made the Hawaiian government anti-American? (Factual.)
7. Was President Harrison right in supporting a treaty of annexation? (Ethical.)
8. Would U.S. national security have been endangered if Hawaii had not been annexed? (Factual.)

Expressing Your Reasoning

1. Should Dole have returned authority to the queen? (In discussing this question, you may wish to have students consider the following

reasons for turning over power: A majority of Hawaiians favored the queen; Blount's report said the revolution was only successful because of the threat of U.S. military force; President Cleveland asked Dole to do so. Reasons for not turning over power include: The queen was not sympathetic to the business leaders; the queen might have retaliated against the people who had brought about the revolution; the United States had previously recognized the provisional government.)

2. Writing assignment: Should the United States have annexed Hawaii? (In discussing students' position papers, you may wish to raise the following considerations: Was the revolution fair? Did most Hawaiians support annexation? Was U.S. national security at stake?)
3. Which group or groups of people should have had the right to vote? (In discussing the voting rights of each group listed in 3.a–3.e on student text page 57, you may wish to have your students identify the pros and cons of each criterion: age, residence, native birth, property held, and literacy. Students may then be asked if any of these criteria should be applied today.)

SINKING INTO WAR
Williams Jennings Bryan

Historical Understanding

1. What was one desire of the Populists? (To reduce the governmental power of wealthy easterners.)
2. In what ways did Germany and England violate America's neutral rights? (Germany sank U.S. ships; England detained U.S. ships that were trying to trade in Europe.)
3. What was *preparedness*? (Preparedness was a policy of military build-up in case of war.)
4. Identify two events that led the United States to enter World War I. (Two crucial events were the sinking of ships by Germany and the Zimmerman note, which indicated that Germany was planning an alliance with Mexico, to facilitate the possible invasion of the United States.)

Reviewing the Facts of the Case

1. What two conditions did President Wilson agree to before William Jennings Bryan was willing to become secretary of state? (The two

conditions were that Bryan would not have to serve alcoholic beverages at diplomatic functions, and that Wilson would work hard for world peace.)

2. How did Bryan and Robert Lansing disagree over what the United States' response should be to the sinking of the *Falaba*? (Lansing believed that Germany should pay for the damages, should punish the submarine commander, and should apologize for the incident. Bryan said that the American should not have been on board and that Germany had given fair warning that the ships were in danger.)
3. In what ways did Wilson and Bryan disagree about what should be done after the sinking of the *Lusitania*? (Bryan sought to maintain neutrality, because he believed that the British were using U.S. lives to protect shipments of ammunition. Therefore Bryan argued that Americans should not be permitted to travel on British ships. Wilson believed that U.S. citizens had the right to free travel and that Germany had made outrageous violations of the neutral rights of the United States.)
4. What did the United States demand from Germany after the sinking of the *Lusitania*? How did Germany respond? (The United States demanded that Germany not use submarines, pay for the loss of life, and prevent any future attacks. Germany said it was acting in self-defense, although it regretted the loss of U.S. lives.)
5. What advice did William McAdoo give Bryan about resignation? (McAdoo said that Bryan should not resign because it would ruin his political career and it would suggest that Americans were deeply divided about the German actions.)
6. What was one reason Bryan resigned? (Bryan believed he was following his conscience.)

Analyzing Ethical Issues

The following are some ethical decisions made in the story: Bryan's decision to continue receiving pay for making speeches; Wilson's decision to enter the war; Bryan's decision to support the U.S. war effort; the British use of neutral flags on ships; Germany's continued use of submarines.

Expressing Your Reasoning

1. Was Bryan right or wrong to resign as secretary of state? (In discussing this question, you may wish to have your students consider the following reasons for resigning: He claimed he was following his conscience; his resignation might persuade others to stay out of the war; he was a pacifist. Reasons against resigning include: He would embarrass

the president; he would hurt his career; his action might encourage Germany to be more aggressive.)

2. Bryan once said that moral principles should regulate the conduct of nations. Indicate whether each of the following activities was right or wrong, and state a principle in support of your judgment. (See the list of activities 1.a–1.e on student text page 68. Among the principles students might be asked to consider are: Civilians should be protected during wartime; nations have a right to self-defense; citizens in a democracy should have the right to travel where they please.)
3. Writing assignment: Do you agree with Theodore Roosevelt that "to be neutral between right and wrong is to serve wrong"? (In discussing students' paragraphs, you may wish to raise the following considerations: If one is truly neutral how can it be said one is serving the wrong? Is it necessary to take a side every time there is a conflict between right and wrong? In moral disagreements is one side always clearly in the right and the other clearly in the wrong? Is the difference between right and wrong one of kind or degree?)

SPEAKING HIS PEACE
Eugene V. Debs

Historical Understanding

1. What was the American Railway Union? (Formed by Debs in 1889, it was a union of all railroad workers.)
2. What do the following terms mean: *scab, yellow-dog contract, injunction,* and *arbitration*? (A scab is a person who takes the job of a striking worker. Yellow-dog contracts were agreements signed by workers saying they would not join a union while employed. An injunction is a court order prohibiting an action. Arbitration is the settling of a dispute by an impartial third party whose decision the disputants agree in advance to accept.)
3. How did the Pullman Strike come to an end? (Federal troops took over the city and the strike was broken.)
4. What did socialists mean by *class struggle*? (It was the idea that the wealthy class would always be at odds with the working class.)
5. How did American socialists differ regarding U.S. involvement in World War I? (Some socialists supported U.S. involvement in the war. Others, like Debs, opposed involvement believing it was an instance of the wealthy class seeking profits at the expense of the working class.)

Reviewing the Facts of the Case

1. How did George Pullman respond to the depression of 1893–1894? (Pullman discharged over one-third of his workers and cut the wages of the others.)
2. Why was Debs jailed during the Pullman strike? (He was convicted of ignoring a court order forbidding any involvement with the strike.)
3. What was the purpose of the Espionage Act? (The Espionage Act made it a crime to speak against or work against United States involvement in World War I.)
4. Why was Debs arrested after his speech in Canton, Ohio? (His speech was held to be a violation of the Espionage Act.)
5. What reasons did President Wilson give for denying a pardon to Debs? (He said Debs was a traitor because he had worked against the war effort after war had been declared by the United States.)

Analyzing Ethical Issues

From Debs' socialist beliefs that are presented in the story, one could reasonably infer whether or not he would find ownership of particular types of private property acceptable. Some inferences are presented below. Students may wish to challenge them with reasoning of their own.

1. A saver's interest on a bank account. (Unacceptable: Debs opposed interest income as unearned.)
2. A union official's salary. (Acceptable: Debs accepted such a salary and never opposed wages for labor.)
3. A person's wristwatch. (Acceptable: Debs owned a watch and did not oppose people owning articles for personal use.)
4. A farmer's land. (Unacceptable: If Debs considered land a means of production like mines, he would want it owned collectively not individually. He would probably not object to a farmer producing food to eat so long as it wasn't sold for profit.)
5. A couple's house. (Acceptable: Debs would probably object to making profits from the sale of real estate but not to owning one's dwelling.)
6. A child's inheritance upon the death of a parent. (Unacceptable: Assuming the inheritance was not earned from the parent's labor, that is, if it were derived from profits, dividends, or interest Debs would object to such a passing down of wealth.)
7. A fisherman's catch. (Acceptable: Debs would probably consider the catch a benefit of one's labor. Selling it for profit would be another matter.)

8. An inventor's patent. (Acceptable/Unacceptable: Debs might approve of some reward for an inventor's labor, but would probably want to limit it according to the amount of work performed.)
9. A landlord's rental income. (Unacceptable: Rental as a form of income from investment would not meet with Debs' approval.)

Expressing Your Reasoning

1. Should Debs have made his Canton, Ohio speech opposing United States involvement in World War I? (Reasons favoring making the speech include: He was doing what he believed in; in a democracy people should be allowed to express their opinions; as a socialist leader he should have the right to try to persuade his party to follow him. Reasons opposing making the speech include: He might be arrested for violating the law; it was wartime and people should not be critical of the war effort; the president of the United States had urged people not to dissent.)
2. The First Amendment of the U.S. Constitution guarantees citizens the right to freedom of speech. Throughout the nation's history there has been debate over the limits of free speech. Should a citizen have a right to:
   a. Criticize a public official. (Yes, could expose incompetence; No, might undermine effectiveness of government.)
   b. Make false statements that harm someone's reputation. (Yes, people must be allowed to speak out and express their beliefs; No, the reputations of innocent people might be damaged.)
   c. Make true statements that damage someone's reputation. (Yes, no one should be prevented from speaking the truth; No, the damage done may outweigh the benefit of knowing the truth.)
   d. Falsely yell "fire" in a crowded theater. (Yes, one restriction on free speech might lead to others; No, speech that presents a clear and present danger to public safety should not be permitted.)
   e. Use obscene language. (Yes, one person's obscenity might be another person's art; No, no one should be compelled to hear language they consider offensive or degrading.)
   f. Urge someone to act violently. (Yes, violent actions can be prohibited without restraining speech; No, people have a right to be protected from provocations that threaten their safety or property.)
   g. Reveal the name of an American secret agent. (Yes, citizens should be allowed to use whatever information they have to protest government policy; No, the life of the agent might be put in jeopardy and national security undermined.)

h. Encourage someone to break a law. (Yes, people should be permitted to urge civil disobedience; No, speech should not be used to incite lawlessness.)

3. Should President Wilson have pardoned Debs when World War I ended? (Reasons favoring the pardon include: It would be an act of mercy; Debs was old and sick and would not be a threat to society; the war was over; others had been pardoned. Reasons opposing the pardon include: Wilson was acting on his sincere belief that a pardon was wrong; lawbreakers should have to serve full sentences; Debs had disobeyed Wilson, so Wilson had no reason to free him.)
4. During the ARU strikes of both the Great Northern Railroad and the Pullman Company, scabs took the jobs of some strikers. Was it right of them to do this? (Reasons favoring scabbing include: They needed the money; they were afraid that a big strike would have hurt the economy and that many people would have suffered; scabs helped keep the companies going; they should have been free to take any job offered by an employer; there was no law against working for less. Reasons against scabbing include: These companies often used blacklists and yellow-dog contracts that were unfair to the workers and scabs should not have supported such owners; scabs might have gotten hurt by the strikers; scabs should have been sympathetic to the union workers and their families; scabs wouldn't have liked the scabbing if they had been union members.)
5. Writing assignment: Some Pullman workers were laid off during the depression. Should the workers who kept their jobs have been willing to accept pay cuts in order to prevent the layoffs? (In discussing students' paragraphs the following reasons could be considered in support of accepting pay cuts to save jobs: During hard times, sacrifices should be shared; if those keeping their jobs were the ones threatened with layoff, they would want other workers to help save their jobs. Reasons against accepting pay cuts include: Those who have been on the job a shorter time can't expect longer term workers to give up pay for them; pay cuts for all would make it hard for everyone to cope; cuts should come from stockholders' profits not workers' wages.)
6. See the summary in the student text, pages 79–80, about the main character, Jean Valjean, in *Les Miserables*.
   a. Should Valjean have stolen the bread from the bakery? (Reasons supporting the theft include: The baker could afford the loss; he thought he wouldn't get caught; Valjean's family was in need; the lives of family members take precedence over the baker's property rights. Reasons opposing the theft include: There was danger of getting caught; he shouldn't make the baker the victim of his family's misfor-

tune; the law against stealing protects everyone's property rights.)

b. The law required a five-year sentence for burglary. Was it right of the judge to sentence Valjean for stealing? (Reasons supporting a sentence include: A judge is obliged to apply the law; other citizens must be discouraged from disobeying the law to solve their problems. Reasons opposing a sentence by the judge include: A judge must balance law with compassion; it is more important for a judge to help alleviate starvation than to uphold the letter of the law—property can't be owned if life is not preserved.)

c. Should the police chief have turned Valjean over to the authorities? (Reasons in support of the police chief's action include: He could satisfy his jealousy; lawbreakers must pay the penalty for their offenses if people are going to respect the law; punishing Valjean might deter other thieves; it is not fair to excuse a crime because the accused is rich and popular. Reasons opposing the police chief's action include: Valjean deserved mercy because his robberies were committed out of his temporary bitterness; Valjean's punishment should be waived because of his good deeds; Valjean had become a model citizen and there was no danger he would commit further crimes.)

Volume 2, Part 2

NORMALCY AND DEPRESSION 1919-1940

BAY STATE BLUES
Boston Police Strike

Historical Understanding

1. What is *inflation*? (Inflation is a continuing rise in the cost of goods and services.)
2. What did workers hope to accomplish by joining unions? (They hoped to improve working conditions and wages.)
3. What is a *general strike*? (It is a strike by all unions, usually as support of one particular union's demands.)
4. How did the Boston police strike help Calvin Coolidge become president? (His strong stand against the police strike was popular among most Americans.)

Reviewing the Facts of the Case

1. What were three job improvements sought by the Boston police? (They wanted their station houses repaired, their wages raised, their working hours lessened, and the right to have a union recognized.)
2. Why did inflation cause special hardships for Boston police? (Police salaries did not go up, while prices for goods and services did.)
3. What were two reasons some people opposed police unions? (Some feared violence would occur if the police went on strike, others feared communists would gain influence in the union, others feared policemen would be unwilling to maintain order if there were strikes by other unions.)
4. What rule did Edwin Curtis make about police unions? (He ruled that no police officers were to join a union.)
5. What recommendations were made by the Storrow Committee? How did Curtis, Peters, and Coolidge react to the recommendations? (The Committee recommended that police officers create a local, nonaffiliated union, that wages and working conditions be investigated, and that no police officer be punished for past involvement in unions. Mayor Peters

approved the committee's ideas, but neither Curtis nor Coolidge approved them.)

6. What specific event triggered the police strike? (Curtis' announcement of the suspension of the policemen involved in union activity.)
7. What was Governor Coolidge's response to Samuel Gompers? (Coolidge said he supported Curtis' decision not to rehire policemen who went on strike. In addition, he said there was no right to strike against the public safety.)

Analyzing Ethical Issues

The following are possible bases for authority that might be claimed for each example:

1. Edwin Curtis ruled that the Boston police were not to join the AFL. (Curtis might claim the authority to issue his rule because he was legally in charge of the police department.)
2. Mayor Peters took charge of the state guardsmen in Boston. (Peters might claim the authority to use the state guard on the basis of the old law that he found.)
3. The Storrow Committee made certain recommendations. (The committee might claim its recommendations should be followed because the members of the Committee represented the citizens of Boston.)
4. Most of the Boston policemen went on strike. (The striking policemen might claim they had the authority to strike because a majority of them voted for the strike.)
5. Governor Coolidge took charge of the state guardsmen in Boston. (Coolidge might claim authority to take charge of the state guard because, as governor, he was constitutionally authorized to do so.)
6. Samuel Gompers sent a telegram to Governor Coolidge on behalf of the AFL. (Gompers might claim the authority to represent the AFL because he had been elected president of that organization.)

Expressing Your Reasoning

1. Should Coolidge have permitted rehiring of the striking policemen? (Among the reasons which might be considered favoring the rehiring are: It would be a humane act of forgiveness; the men were already trained as skilled policemen; they had suffered long enough. Reasons against rehiring include: They had disobeyed authority; they might strike again; the public opposed the strike.)

2. Writing assignment: Should the Boston police have gone on strike? (In discussing students' position papers, you may wish to raise the following considerations for striking: A majority voted for it; other workers had better wages; they had tried other ways to achieve their aims. Against striking: They were ordered not to join a union; violence might follow; the public opposed the strike.)
3. Would it be wrong for nurses, trash collectors, air traffic controllers, soldiers, and doctors to strike? (In discussing this question, you may wish to have students identify the public safety services of each group, that is, health, prevention of disease, prevention of airplane accidents, and national security. If students think it acceptable for some to strike but not others, they should explain why one public service is more vital than another.)

STEALING NORTH
Richard Wright

Historical Understanding

1. What was Abraham Lincoln's position on racial equality before the Civil War? (Before the Civil War, Lincoln believed that whites were superior to blacks, and he opposed all forms of racial equality.)
2. What were the two major purposes of Jim Crow laws? (Jim Crow laws were designed to segregate the races and to keep blacks in an inferior position.)
3. Give three specific examples of Jim Crow laws. (Three examples of Jim Crow laws are: denial of the vote to blacks, separate schools for blacks and whites, and no contests between sports teams of different races.)
4. What precedent was set by the case of *Plessy* v. *Ferguson*? ("Separate but equal" was the precedent set by the case of *Plessy* v. *Ferguson*. According to the decision, states could constitutionally segregate the races if their separate facilities were equal.)

Reviewing the Facts of the Case

1. Why did Richard quit his job doing chores for a white family? (Richard quit his job doing chores because his white woman employer fed him spoiled food and insulted him.)

2. For what purpose was Richard trying to save money? (Richard was trying to save money for train fare to the North.)
3. How was Richard treated by the owner of the brickyard? (When the brickyard owner's dog bit Richard, the owner refused to be concerned about the injury saying, "A dog bite can't hurt a nigger.")
4. Why was Richard fired from the clothing store? (Richard was fired from the clothing store because he would not act servile and happy, as expected of blacks by the white employer.)
5. What agreement did Richard reach with the theater owner? (The theater owner and Richard pledged to be honest with each other.)
6. Describe how the ticket scheme worked. (The ticket scheme enabled Richard and other theater employees to embezzle money. As ticket taker, Richard set aside some of the tickets he took from customers and sent them by courier back to the ticket window to be sold again. Proceeds from the duplicate sale of tickets were divided among the schemers.)

Analyzing Ethical Issues

The following are examples of racial discrimination resulting from either government or private actions:

1. A restaurant hires white waitresses only. (Private action.)
2. An athletic club excludes whites from membership. (Private action.)
3. A school board requires black and white children to attend separate schools. (Government action.)
4. Prisoners in a state prison are segregated by race. (Government action.)
5. A city police department favors black job applicants. (Government action.)
6. A religious group excludes blacks from its clergy. (Private action.)
7. The Navy hires only black cooks. (Government action.)
8. A landlord rents to whites only. (Private action.)
9. A county board accepts bids to build a new office building only from black-owned construction firms. (Government action.)

Students are asked to cite from the story one example of discrimination by government action and one by private action. An example of discrimination by government action is the Louisiana law requiring separate railway cars for whites and blacks. An example of discrimination by private individuals is lynching of black World War I veterans. Students may cite numerous other examples from the story.

Expressing Your Reasoning

1. Should Richard have participated in the ticket scheme? (Reasons supporting Richard's decision to participate in the ticket scheme include: It was a way of getting even with whites who had mistreated him; he got the money for train fare to the North where he could become a writer; he could escape the racial discrimination of the Jim Crow South and send for his family later; the scheme helped other black employees get extra money; Richard had no obligation to obey the Mississippi law against stealing passed by a Jim Crow legislature because the law was adopted without consent of the governed. Reasons opposing Richard's decision include: If caught, he would be sent to a chain gang; he was stealing from a person who had treated him decently; it would be disappointing to his family for Richard to become known as a thief; he broke his promise to be honest; the law against stealing protects everyone's property. *Note:* The teacher may wish to ask whether students' judgments of Richard's action would be different if the theater owner were black.)
2. Suppose that before Richard joined in the ticket scheme the owner had approached him and asked if he knew whether anything dishonest was happening among the employees. Would it have been right for Richard to tell the theater owner about the ticket scheme and who was involved in it? (Some of the reasons presented for question 1 above could be weaved into discussion of this point. Additional reasons, both in favor and against Richard's telling the truth, could also be raised for consideration. In favor: He might gain the trust and confidence of the theater owner and thereby get favored treatment from him; by exposing the others he might help deter them from further stealing; the owner's property rights were at stake—if Richard owned the theater, he would want to be informed of fraud by employees. Against: He was willing to take the chance of getting caught and to accept the consequences; his friends might be harshly punished; he would be betraying members of his race in a society divided by race.)
3. Refer to the short story, "Mrs. Webster's Rooming House," on student text page 103. Was it wrong of Mrs. Webster to reject Mr. Jones? (In discussing students' written judgments of Mrs. Webster's decision, you may wish to raise the following reasons in support of her decision: Accepting Mr. Jones would threaten her only source of income; she should be allowed to control access to her own property; people should not go where they are not welcome. Reasons opposing Mrs. Webster's decision include: Bigotry is wrong—people should be judged individually and not by membership in a racial or ethnic group; it was wrong to lie to

Mr. Jones; access to public accommodations should not be restricted by race. *Legal note:* Under the federal 1968 Fair Housing Act, Mrs. Webster's rental discrimination would be unlawful discrimination on the basis of race if there were four or more units in her rooming house. State law may offer greater protection to tenants.)

REBEL WITHOUT A PAUSE
Zelda Fitzgerald

Historical Understanding

1. What were the provisions of the Eighteenth and Nineteenth Amendments? (The Eighteenth prohibited the sale, manufacture, or transportation of alcoholic beverages; the Nineteenth granted women the right to vote.)
2. Name three forms of entertainment popular in the 1920s. (Movies, radio, sports, going to nightclubs.)
3. What were two ways in which women of the 1920s rebelled against tradition? (They rebelled by smoking and drinking in public and by wearing revealing clothing.)
4. What was *bootlegging*? What were *speakeasies*? (Bootlegging was the practice of illegally smuggling and selling liquor. Speakeasies were illegal nightclubs where alcohol was served.)

Reviewing the Facts of the Case

1. What were Zelda's ideas about how flappers should live? (She said they should experiment with life, rebel against tradition, and do things they enjoyed.)
2. What were three characteristics of Zelda that Scott adored? (He adored her beauty, courage, sincerity, and self-respect.)
3. Identify two things that Zelda did that showed she rebelled against tradition. (She smoked and drank in public, went bathing while pregnant, and broke a store window because she impulsively wanted a picture that was in the store.)
4. Why did Scott not want Zelda to sell her diary? (He used her entries for ideas for his stories.)
5. What did Zelda's doctor urge Scott to do when Zelda wanted to know her chances of becoming a great dancer? (He did not want her to know that she could have some success as a dancer because he believed her obsession was prolonging her illness.)

6. Why was Scott angry with Zelda about the writing of her novel? (He believed she had used some of his ideas and writing in her work.)

Analyzing Ethical Issues

An incident from the story involving the value of truth was Scott and the doctor's withholding from Zelda the information from her dance teacher.

Expressing Your Reasoning

1. Should Zelda have stopped writing because Scott demanded it? (In discussing this question, you may wish to have your students consider the following: The fact that they were married; the problems Scott was having in finishing his work because of taking care of her; the possibility that she was using some of his ideas in her writing; the possibility that writing might be therapeutic for her.)
2. Was it wrong of Scott to mislead Zelda about her teacher's opinion of her dancing ability? (Among the reasons that might be considered for withholding the information are: Zelda's doctor thought she should not be told; it might have been in Zelda's best interests for her husband to do whatever he thought was best for her. Some reasons against withholding the information are: Knowing her teacher's opinion might have made her feel better; she had a general right to know the truth; as her husband, Scott should have done as Zelda asked. Students are also asked if there are any circumstances in which patients should not be told the truth.)
3. Writing assignment: Was it wrong to go to illegal nightclubs? (In discussing students' paragraphs, you may wish to raise the following considerations: The nightclubs were illegal; people who went to speak-easies could get arrested; many people were doing the same thing; many people thought they had the right to do as they pleased.)

BAD NEWS
Near v. Minnesota

Historical Understanding

1. Identify two effects the discovery of iron ore had on the city of Duluth. (It created a wealthy class of shippers and mine owners. Gamblers and gangsters came to town to make money from the workers.)

2. What were the provisions of the Eighteenth Amendment? How did it contribute to an increase in crime? (The Eighteenth Amendment prohibited the sale, manufacture, and transportation of alcoholic beverages. Gangsters violated the law and supplied liquor to those who sought it.)
3. What is meant by *prior restraint*? (It is a form of censorship in which publications are kept from printing stories.)

Reviewing the Facts of the Case

1. How did the publication of the *Rip-saw* lead to the 1925 Public Nuisance Law? (*Rip-saw* printed scandalous and sometimes libelous stories that injured the reputations of leading citizens.)
2. What were the provisions of the 1925 Public Nuisance Law? (Publishers who knowingly printed false and damaging stories could be told to cease publication.)
3. Why did gangsters attack Sam Shapiro? (He refused to deal with mobsters who tried to shut down his cleaning business.)
4. Why did Floyd Olson try to shut down the *Saturday Press*? (The paper printed insulting charges against him.)
5. Why did the Minnesota Supreme Court say the 1925 law was constitutional? (It said freedom of the press does not mean that everything can be published. Limits may be set on freedom of the press.)
6. Why did Colonel McCormick want to take Near's case to the Supreme Court of the United States? (McCormick wanted the Court to make a strong statement favoring freedom of the press. He feared that many states might try to follow the example of Minnesota's Public Nuisance Law.)

Analyzing Ethical Issues

The following questions are either factual or ethical:

1. Would Near have won his case without McCormick's support? (Factual.)
2. Should the *Saturday Press* have been forced to stop publishing? (Ethical.)
3. Should Shapiro have resisted Barnett's demands? (Ethical.)
4. Would most people sue newspapers that insulted their reputations? (Factual.)

5. Was it fair of Near to charge that Olson cooperated with gangsters? (Ethical.)

Some other factual issues in the story are: Whether or not Barnett arranged for the shooting of Near's partner; whether or not most of Near's stories were untrue; whether or not crime would have increased if the Eighteenth Amendment had not been passed.

Some other ethical issues in the story are: Whether or not the Minnesota law should have been passed; whether or not Guilford should have identified his attackers; whether or not the Supreme Court should have upheld the Minnesota Law.

Expressing Your Reasoning

1. Should prejudiced people like Jay Near be allowed to publish papers like the *Saturday Press*? (Among the arguments that might be considered in favor of permitting publication are: If lies are printed the publishers can be sued; in a democracy the need for freedom of the press is so great that virtually anything should be allowed to be published; the public is wise enough to know when bigotry is being published. Among arguments that might be considered opposing publication are: Publishers should have an obligation to print the truth for good purposes; the public might take violent action if malicious stories are printed; stopping sleazy publications is no threat to freedom of the press.)
2. Would it be wrong to print the truth in various circumstances? (See the circumstances 2.a–2.d on student text page 121. In the discussion, students should consider the following criteria: the reputation of a respected citizen, national security, a prior promise not to publish, and the right to a fair trial.)
3. Writing assignment: Should the U.S. Supreme Court have upheld the Minnesota Public Nuisance Law? (Among the reasons for upholding the law which might be considered are: The law was favored by a majority of Minnesota legislators and publishers; the law only affected publishers who intentionally printed false and insulting stories; permitting scandal sheets to publish might cause those who are defamed to seek violent revenge. Among the reasons for overturning the law which might be considered are: In a democracy freedom of the press should be interpreted as broadly as possible; the law did not call for a jury trial so it gave too much power to a single judge; those who suffered at the hands of a scandal sheet could sue the publisher.)

SOLDIERS OF MISFORTUNE
Bonus Army

Historical Understanding

1. Identify three effects of the Great Depression. (Massive unemployment, falling farm prices, bank failures, loss of homes, and business failures were among the effects of the Depression.)
2. What did Congress provide World War I veterans in 1924? (The law provided medical and other benefits for veterans and authorized a payment of money in 1945.)
3. Why were many Washington authorities worried about Communists? (They feared the Communists might attempt a violent overthrow of the government.)

Reviewing the Facts of the Case

1. Why did the Bonus Army come to Washington? (Members of the Bonus Army sought an early payment of their bonuses.)
2. In what way did Chief Glassford and the district commissioners disagree on how the Bonus Army should be treated? (Glassford favored treating the Bonus Army kindly to keep it under control. The district commissioners wanted the veterans moved out of the city, by force if necessary.)
3. What did Glassford do to help maintain order during the stay of the Bonus Army? (He worked closely with the leaders of the Bonus Army and helped the veterans obtain food and shelter.)
4. What were two arguments in favor of the bonus bill and two arguments against it? (Supporters said that the veterans deserved the money and that the payments might help to stimulate the economy. Opponents said that the nation could not afford the payments and that other unemployed citizens were not getting payments.)
5. What was Walter Waters' attitude toward Communists? (Waters did not want Communists in the ranks of the Bonus Army.)
6. Why did Washington officials want the Bonus Army to leave after the Senate voted against the bonus? (The officials did not think they could afford to house and feed the veterans and also wanted to proceed with plans to demolish old buildings in which some of the veterans were staying.)
7. Why were federal troops called out? (Violence broke out between the police and some of the veterans.)

8. How did General MacArthur and President Hoover differ on how troops should be used? (Hoover wanted minimum force to be used and the veterans moved only out of the downtown area. MacArthur wanted the veterans driven completely out of the city.)

Analyzing Ethical Issues

Some other decision topics with related factual and ethical issues are:

Glassford's decision to work with the Bonus Army. *Factual issue:* Would kindness be effective at maintaining control? *Ethical issue:* Should Glassford have followed the preferences of his superiors?)

MacArthur's decision to drive the veterans out of Anacostia. *Factual issue:* Would the veterans have returned to the downtown area if they were not driven out? *Ethical issue:* Should MacArthur have exceeded the president's orders?

Expressing Your Reasoning

1. Should the Bonus Army have been driven out of the capital? (Among the reasons which might be considered favoring driving out the Bonus Army are: They were preventing demolition workers from doing their job; Glassford had urged them to leave; the Congress was not going to pass the bonus bill; it was the only way to get them out. Reasons not to drive them out include: It was too harsh; they were veterans and deserved better treatment; as citizens they should have had the right to demonstrate.)
2. Should Waters have tried to keep the veterans in Washington? (Among the reasons favoring his action are: Perhaps a new demonstration could have brought passage of the bonus bill; if the veterans left, they would have had no chance of receiving their payment; as their leader, Waters should have done all he could to help. Reasons opposing his action include: The bill had failed; Glassford and others had asked the veterans to leave; he could no longer have hoped for passage of the bill.)
3. Writing assignment: Should the president have punished MacArthur for disobedience? (In discussing students' paragraphs, you may wish to raise the following considerations: By punishing MacArthur, it might have appeared that Hoover was trying to shift blame from himself; by not punishing him, MacArthur might have disobeyed orders again; as commander of the armed forces, Hoover had an obligation to punish any soldier who disobeyed him; MacArthur had gotten the job done and that accomplishment was in the best interests of the country.)

4. Which, if any, types of benefits should veterans receive? (See 4.a–4.d on student text page 131 for the list of possible benefits. In discussing this question, you may wish your students to consider: Whether veterans should receive benefits that other citizens do not; whether the benefit should be related exclusively to the effects of military action—injury-related, for example—as opposed to more general benefits, such as payment for education.)

UNITED WE SIT
Flint Sit-down Strike

Historical Understanding

1. During the 1930s, what was the leading industry in the United States and which corporation was the largest manufacturer in that industry? (Automobile manufacturing was the largest industry and General Motors was the largest manufacturer.)
2. In a labor dispute, what is *arbitration*? (Arbitration is the settling of disputes by an impartial third party whose decision disputants agree in advance to accept.)
3. What were two goals of the UAW in the 1930s? (The UAW sought to gain recognition as the only labor union for autoworkers and to improve the hours, wages, and working conditions for autoworkers.)
4. What were the major provisions of the National Labor Relations Act of 1935? (The NLRA required employers to bargain with their workers; prohibited unfair labor practices, such as firing union members and interfering with union organizing efforts, and allowed workers to vote for the specific union that they wanted to represent them.)

Reviewing the Facts of the Case

1. What was GM's policy toward labor unions during the 1930s? (General Motors refused to deal formally with labor unions.)
2. Identify two complaints autoworkers had about their jobs. (Autoworkers complained about the speed of the assembly line, lay-off procedures, the long working hours, and safety conditions.)
3. Why did the UAW choose Flint as the location for the sit-down strike? (Flint was the site of the largest auto body factory in the world, and most of the workers in the city were autoworkers.)
4. Why was the sit-down type of strike chosen as a tactic by the

UAW? (The tactic of the sit-down strike, with workers remaining at their machines, made the company reluctant to use force for fear of damaging the machines. In addition, by staying in the plants, workers made it difficult for the company to hire new workers to replace the strikers.)

5. In what ways did Governor Murphy influence the outcome of the GM sit-down strike? (The governor worked hard for a negotiated settlement between GM and the UAW; he refused to use troops to break the strike, and he allowed welfare payments to strikers.)
6. What effects did the GM sit-down strike have upon (a) the organized labor movement and (b) Frank Murphy's political career? (As a result of the strike, organized labor became stronger and many more workers joined unions, especially the UAW; Governor Murphy was not reelected largely because of his sympathy toward the strikers.)

Analyzing Ethical Issues

Among the incidents involving the value of property are: The strikers occupying the plant owned by General Motors; the state paying welfare benefits to strikers, and the workers threatening to destroy factory machinery if attempts were made to remove them by force.

Expressing Your Reasoning

1. Should Governor Murphy have forcibly ejected the sit-down strikers from the plants they occupied in Flint? (See 2.a–2.h on student text page 143 for a list of facts to be taken into account when judging Murphy's decision.)
2. Which should have been the most and least important reasons to the governor in deciding whether to use force to evict the strikers? (Refer again to the list of facts 2.a–2.h for the possible choices. Most students will be able to identify some reasons as more persuasive than others. They often have difficulty, however, articulating criteria that lie behind their selection of one reason over another. Establishing such criteria requires a sophisticated intellectual effort in ethical philosophy. It is unreasonable to expect students to pursue the ethical adequacy of reasons in great depth. They can, however, be introduced to the general problem of seeking criteria for justification.

   After students have identified some reasons as better than others, they should be asked to explain why they made their selections. After eliciting their explanations, you may wish to list the following ways in which reasons may be characterized:

A reason that emphasizes revenge against an offending party
A reason that stresses the self-interest of one party in the dispute
A reason that stresses the need to show compassion for one or more of the parties involved
A reason that emphasizes following custom or tradition
A reason that shows respect for legitimate authority
A reason that shows concern for the welfare of society as a whole
A reason that attempts to take into account the rights of all parties concerned

Students may be asked if any of the above characterizations fit the reasons they selected. You may then discuss whether some of these types of reasons should be preferred over others. For example: Is a reason that shows respect for the rule of law better than one that focuses on revenge?)

3. Writing assignment: Would it be fair for GM to follow a seniority system in determining layoffs, as the workers wanted them to? (In discussing students' written paragraphs about the fairness of a seniority system, you may wish to have students ponder the following: Under the proposed seniority system, management might have to let some of the best workers go; by keeping workers with less time of service, management could pay less in wages, and thereby keep prices lower; if minorities had been last hired, they would be first fired; it is harder for older workers to find new jobs; older workers tend to have more family financial responsibilities. You may want to ask students what criterion ought to be used for layoffs if not seniority.)
4. During the sit-down strike in Flint, Governor Murphy ordered that public relief be paid by the state government to nonstrikers and strikers alike. Do you think he was right to grant welfare payments to the families of striking workers? (Reasons supporting welfare payments include: The strikers' families were in need; strikers should not be the victims of management's refusal to bargain. Reasons opposing welfare payments include: Tax money should not be used to support either side during a strike; the strikers chose to strike and must accept the consequences.)

YEARNING TO BREATHE FREE
Jewish Refugees

Historical Understanding

1. Identify three ways the Nazi government discriminated against Jews during the 1930s. (Jews were not permitted to hold certain jobs, their

property was taken, they were kept from certain public facilities, and their citizenship was taken away.)

2. What were the major provisions of the 1924 National Origins Immigration Act? (The act set quotas on the number of persons who could emigrate from each nation. The highest quotas were for persons from Northern and Western Europe; no immigrants from Asia were permitted.)
3. Define the following terms: *isolationist, nativist, anti-Semite,* and *restrictionist.* (Isolationists were those who believed that the United States should not be involved in world affairs. Nativists were those who looked down on immigrants and opposed immigration. Anti-Semites were those who were hostile toward or discriminated against Jews. Restrictionists were those who wanted strict limits set on immigration or all immigration to be outlawed.)

Reviewing the Facts of the Case

1. Approximately how many Germans could legally immigrate to the United States each year during the 1930s? (The German yearly quota was about 26,000 persons.)
2. What action did President Roosevelt take after hearing of *Kristallnacht*? (He spoke out against the brutality and extended the visitor's visas of visiting German Jews for six months.)
3. Why were the Cuban visas invalidated? (President Bru discovered that the visas were fraudulent.)
4. How did the Nazi government make use of the voyage of the *St. Louis* for propaganda purposes? (The Nazis said that the fact that many nations refused to accept the Jewish refugees showed that Germany was not the only nation that did not want Jews within its borders.)
5. What was the official position of the U.S. Department of State regarding the refugee passengers? (The State Department said that it was a problem between Cuba and the refugees.)
6. What was Hitler's "final solution"? (The "final solution" was the systematic extermination of the Jewish population.)

Analyzing Ethical Issues

The following are some incidents involving the identified values:

The value of authority was involved when President Roosevelt would not overturn the State Department's ruling.

The value of life was involved when the "final solution" was adopted.

Expressing Your Reasoning

1. Should President Roosevelt have admitted the passengers aboard the *St. Louis* into the United States? (See the two lists of considerations in 2.a–2.e on student text pages 153–154.)
2. Which reasons are most persuasive? (Refer again to the lists 2.a–2.e on student text pages 153–154. Most students will be able to identify some reasons as more persuasive than others. They often have difficulty, however, articulating criteria that lie behind their selection of one reason over another. Establishing such criteria requires a sophisticated intellectual effort in ethical philosophy. It is unreasonable to expect students to pursue the ethical adequacy of reasons in great depth. They can, however, be introduced to the general problem of seeking criteria for justification.

   After students have identified some reasons as better than others, they should be asked to explain why they made their selections. After eliciting their explanations, you may wish to list the following ways in which reasons may be characterized:

   A reason that emphasizes revenge against an offending party
   A reason that stresses the self-interest of one party in the dispute
   A reason that stresses the need to show compassion for one or more of the parties involved
   A reason that emphasizes following custom or tradition
   A reason that shows respect for legitimate authority
   A reason that shows concern for the welfare of society as a whole
   A reason that attempts to take into account the rights of all parties concerned

   Students may be asked if any of the above characterizations fit the reasons they selected. You may then discuss whether some of these types of reasons should be preferred over others. For example: Is a reason that shows respect for the rule of law better than one that focuses on revenge?)
3. Writing assignment: Create an immigration policy. (See considerations 3.a–3.h on student text page 154. In discussing students' policies, you may wish to raise the following points: Whether the characteristic is changeable, for example, the ability to speak English, or unchangeable, for example, the person's age or whether he or she has job skills that immediately qualify the person for a job; whether the hiring of the person would prevent a U.S. citizen from getting the job; whether the person is fleeing political persecution in a nondemocratic nation: You may also wish to discuss the idea of the United States as a traditional haven for immigrants.)

Volume 2, Part 3
HOT AND COLD WAR
1941-1960

A LOADED WEAPON
Japanese Relocation

Historical Understanding

1. Why did Japanese-Americans become unpopular along the West Coast? (They were willing to work for low wages, which threatened unions, and their success as farmers was resented by local growers. Some whites disliked the Japanese because of their race.)
2. What were the major terms of the 1907 "Gentlemen's Agreement"? (The Japanese government agreed to reduce immigration to the United States. The United States government agreed not to adopt laws that discriminated against Japanese in the United States.)
3. Why were the Nisei citizens of the United States, but not their parents? (The Nisei were born in the United States and therefore citizens according to the U.S. Constitution. The Issei, as immigrants from Asia were, according to a federal law passed in 1790, "aliens ineligible to citizenship." This law was changed in the 1950s.)
4. What was meant by the phrase *yellow peril*? (This term was popularized by some California newspapers in 1905 after Japan's defeat of Russia. It referred to a fear by some whites that waves of Japanese immigrants would engulf the state of California.)
5. Define the following terms: *espionage, sabotage,* and *fifth column.* (Espionage is spying by enemy agents to obtain government secrets; sabotage is the destruction of property by enemy agents, and a fifth column is a secret organization, within a country, that aids an invading enemy.)

Reviewing the Facts of the Case

1. What were Executive Order 9066 and Public Law 503? (Executive Order 9066, issued in February 1942 by President Roosevelt, gave the

army the authority to move civilians out of western coastal states. Though it encompassed all civilians who might affect the war effort, it was intended for and used only in relation to Japanese-Americans. Public Law 503 was an act of Congress, passed in March 1942, which endorsed the executive order and provided for its enforcement in the federal courts. Fred Korematsu was prosecuted for violating this law.)

2. What reasons were given by the U.S. government for evacuating Japanese-Americans from the Pacific Coast? (Five major reasons were given by the government: (1) Japanese-Americans posed a threat as enemy agents; (2) evacuation would raise morale of whites living on the West Coast; (3) evacuating the Japanese would protect them from attack by hostile citizens; (4) the loyalty of some Japanese was doubtful, and there was no convenient way to distinguish the loyal from the disloyal; (5) in total war, constitutional rights must yield to drastic measures for protection of national security.)
3. Briefly summarize conditions at Tanforen and Topaz. (The centers were surrounded by barbed wire and guarded by armed soldiers; quarters were crude and cramped; food was of low quality; there was little privacy and few comforts; residents were permitted limited self-government; churches, schools, hospitals, and recreation programs were set up; and some residents received low-paying jobs. Generally, life in the relocation camps was dreary, stark, and isolated.)
4. What was the majority decision in the case of *Korematsu* v. *United States*? (In a 6 to 3 decision, the majority of justices of the U.S. Supreme Court upheld the conviction of Fred Korematsu for violating a civilian exclusion order. According to the decision, the evacuation and relocation of Japanese-Americans did not violate their constitutional rights.)
5. What do the three dissenting opinions in the Korematsu case have in common? (The three dissenting justices all claimed that it is a violation of constitutional rights to imprison someone because of his or her race.)

Analyzing Ethical Issues

Following are three incidents from the story involving the value of equality and the groups that were treated differently in these incidents:

In 1906 the San Francisco School Board established separate schools for Japanese children.—Japanese children, white children

In 1790 Congress passed a law limiting citizenship to "free white persons."—Free whites and nonwhites

In 1924 immigration of Asians to the United States was halted.—Asians and people from other continents

Students may discover other incidents in the story involving the value of equality.

Expressing Your Reasoning

1. Did the U.S. government do the right thing when it evacuated Americans of Japanese ancestry from the Pacific Coast during World War II? (Students could be asked to consider the following reasons given by the government to justify the evacuation: There was danger of espionage and sabotage; it protected the Japanese from those hostile to them; some Japanese were loyal to Japan, and the loyal could not easily be distinguished from the disloyal. Additional arguments include the Supreme Court majority view of Justice Black: Military urgency required extraordinary security measures; courts should not second-guess military decisions. Students who argue that the evacuation was the right thing to do could be asked whether Americans of German and Italian ancestry should also have been evacuated.

   For reasons against the evacuation, students could examine the main points of the dissenting Supreme Court opinion: The Constitution protects citizens from confinement on the basis of their ancestry; it is wrong to deprive people of their rights on the basis of race, including the right to live and work where they choose, and to move about freely. Students who argue that the evacuation was the wrong thing to do could be asked: What if there had been proof of espionage and sabotage? Would the threat of immediate danger to all have justified suspension of liberty for some?)
2. Writing assignment: Was Fred Korematsu wrong to resist the evacuation order? (In discussing students' paragraphs, you may wish to raise reasons both supporting and opposing what Korematsu did. Supporting: He was loyal to the United States and not a threat to national security; he had a commitment to his fiancée; if he thought the law was unjust, he should not comply with it, which is an act of civil disobedience; he owed nothing to a society that discriminated against him because of his race. Opposing: By obeying the order he could avoid the draft; if he wanted to disobey, he should have accepted the consequences and not tried to sneak around them by disguising his ancestry; he was disgracing his own people

by breaking the law and making a bad situation worse for them; in a national emergency everyone should cooperate with the authorities.)

3. For each situation below, indicate whether or not you think *equal protection of the law* is being denied. Be prepared to state reasons for your judgments. (The law can be taken into account as one consideration in making a judgment. For each situation, current federal law is presented first and then some ethical considerations for evaluating the fairness of the law)
   a. A landlord refuses to rent an apartment to Vietnamese immigrants. (This action is unlawful under the Civil Rights Act of 1968, which prohibits discrimination based on race, color, religion, or national origin in the sale or rental of most housing. Students could be asked whether this law treats the property rights of landlords fairly, that is, whether or not landlords should be allowed to rent to whomever they please.)
   b. Persons under age 18 are refused admittance to movie theaters showing X-rated films. (Discrimination based on age for admission to films has been upheld as lawful by courts. Students could be asked to distinguish between fair and unfair age discrimination.)
   c. A private club denies membership to blacks. (The Supreme Court decided in *Moose Lodge* v. *Irvis* (1972) that a private club could restrict its membership. Because there is no state action, this restriction is not prohibited by the equal protection clause of the Fourteenth Amendment to the Constitution. Students could be asked to consider whether individuals have a right to discriminate on the basis of race in their private lives, for example, in choosing friends or selecting the members of clubs.)
   d. Because of their religion, high school–age Amish children are not required to comply with a state compulsory school attendance law. (The Supreme Court ruled in 1972 that in the case of the Amish, the right to free exercise of one's religion was more important than the two years of required schooling. Students could be asked to consider whether religious liberty is a good reason to make an exception to the school attendance law. They could also consider what influence the Amish children ought to have in the matter.)
   e. Men are required to register for military service. (This is current federal law. Students could consider whether men and women should be treated differently for purposes of military service.)
   f. A commercial airline requires pilots to retire upon reaching age 50. (Courts have upheld forced retirement in cases where persons lose certain reflexes as they get older and may endanger the safety of themselves or others. Students could consider whether or

not, when deciding upon retirement, it is fair to judge people by age or by individual performance.)

g. Auto insurance rates are higher for people who are young and unmarried. (The law permits this practice. Students could consider whether it is fair to treat people as members of an age group. In this example, they could weigh the fact that young and unmarried drivers, on the average, have more auto accidents.)

h. In some states people under age 21 are not permitted to purchase alcoholic beverages. (This is lawful. Students could consider whether it is fair to set a minimum age for some activities. In this example, it is drinking. Other examples could include voting, school attendance, marriage, and being held responsible for contracts.)

i. A school district has separate schools for black and white students. (This practice was found unconstitutional by the Supreme Court in *Brown* v. *Board of Education* (1954). The Court said that racially separate schools were "inherently unequal." Students could be asked to consider whether this ruling should apply to private schools. They could also consider whether steps should be taken to change the racial makeup of schools where there has been past racial discrimination.)

j. A state university reserves some places in its freshmen medical school class for minority students. (In the case of *Bakke* v. *The University of California* (1978), the Supreme Court held that special racial quotas were illegal, but that race could be considered as one factor in admitting students to schools seeking a diverse student body. Students could be asked to consider the fairness of "reverse discrimination," that is, affirmative action programs intended to remedy the effects of past discrimination. This issue is raised in greater detail in a subsequent episode in Part 4 of this book: "Affirmative or Negative.")

4. Some people argue that evacuation of Japanese-Americans was the right thing to do at the time, but that it seems wrong looking back from the present time. Can an action be both right and wrong depending upon when the judgment about it is made? Explain your thinking. (This question raises the concept of ethical relativism—the notion that any action can be either right or wrong depending on where it takes place, when it takes place, or who is involved. Relativism can be questioned by asking students whether there are any ethical rules that should always apply. If so, what is an example of one? The Golden Rule—"Do unto others as you would have them do unto you"—could be raised for consideration. Could Japanese relocation have been justified under the Golden Rule? If students claim there are no universal ethical rules, they can be asked how to judge right from wrong without them.)

ABOUT FACE
General Joseph Stilwell

Historical Understanding

1. What was the general strategy of the United States at the beginning of World War II? (The general strategy was to first win the war in Europe and then fight in Asia where Jiang Jie-shi [Chiang Kai-shek] was to have kept the Japanese Army occupied.)
2. Why did President Roosevelt want to keep China in the war? (Japanese troops could not invade Australia and other nations if they were kept busy fighting the Chinese.)
3. What was the Lend-Lease Act? (It was a program of military aid from the United States to nations fighting its enemies.)
4. Identify a political and a cultural factor that kept Jiang Jie-shi from pursuing the war in the way preferred by the United States. (A political factor was the fact that Jiang did not have the full support of his troops and those of the Communists; a cultural factor was a Chinese tradition of avoiding direct combat and holding back troops.)

Reviewing the Facts of the Case

1. What is meant by the Chinese tradition of *saving face*? (It meant that one had to keep up appearances of dignity and politeness in all situations.)
2. What was the difference between Stilwell's opinion of Chinese soldiers and their officers? (He believed the soldiers could be made into an effective fighting force but that their officers were often incompetent and corrupt.)
3. Why was the Burma Road militarily important? (It was the major supply route into China.)
4. Stilwell recommended reforms to strengthen the Chinese army. Why did Jiang reject Stilwell's ideas? (He rejected the reforms because some of the officers in his army might use the strengthened troops to overthrow him.)
5. Why did President Roosevelt want to give Jiang the Legion of Merit? (It was a way to honor Jiang and keep him fighting the Japanese.)
6. Why did Jiang reject Roosevelt's request that Stilwell be made commander of the Chinese army? (He rejected it partly because he feared the Communists would become part of the regular Chinese army.)

Analyzing Ethical Issues

Another instance in which Stilwell understood Jiang's actions but did not think them justified was: Stilwell understood that Jiang's need to save face and his fears of officers turning against him were reasons why Jiang would not accept reforms of his army. Stilwell believed Jiang's actions were wrong, because they prolonged the war and prevented an effective war against the Japanese.

Expressing Your Reasoning

1. Should President Roosevelt have recalled Stilwell from China? (Among the reasons that might be considered for withdrawing Stilwell are: He had insulted Jiang; Jiang, as a leader of China, did not want to have to deal with Stilwell; Stilwell was ineffective in dealing with Jiang. Reasons not to withdraw Stilwell include: He had proven he could be an effective leader when given authority to do so; winning the war was more important than pleasing Jiang; Jiang had originally agreed that Stilwell could command Chinese troops and then backed out of his agreement. *Although not mentioned in the story, Roosevelt did recall Stilwell.*)
2. Try to explain how each of the following cultural practices may have come about. Then decide whether or not each is justifiable.
   a. A thief in Arabia is convicted for the second time and has his hand chopped off as punishment. (An eye-for-an-eye type of punishment may be customary.)
   b. In a harsh arctic climate, an old woman, who can no longer contribute to the survival of the tribe, is left on the ice to die. (In such harsh conditions, if one member of the group cannot contribute, all might suffer or die.)
   c. On a tiny Pacific island, stealing is customary. A person will pretend to be friendly with someone and then take his or her possessions when the opportunity arises. (There may be no tradition of private property on the island.)
   d. People in one culture worship cattle as sacred. Even if they are starving they will not kill cattle for food. (They may believe that they will be rewarded in an afterlife if they follow their religion strictly.)
   e. In some cultures, people cannot marry whom they choose. Parents decide whom their children must marry. (Marriages may be seen as opportunities to create political or economic ties with other families and not a matter of love.)
3. Writing assignment: Is it justifiable to judge the rightness or wrongness

of practices in other cultures? (In discussing students' paragraphs, you may wish to raise the following considerations: Are we willing to allow people from other cultures to judge our practices? Are some behaviors so heinous, for example, torture, murder, head-hunting, that they cannot be justified? Should people from other cultures who come to the United States be allowed to follow their cultural practices even if they violate U.S. law or custom? You may also wish to have students consider what constitutes a culture and whether there are complete subcultures within the United States.)

THE UNLUCKIEST KID
Private Eddie Slovik

Historical Understanding

1. What was General Patton's worry as the country prepared for war? (He worried about whether American young people would be capable of fighting with the necessary courage.)
2. How did war contribute to Detroit's economy? (The economy was helped because of the manufacture of needed military equipment.)
3. What was D day? (June 6, 1944 was the date that Allied forces landed at Normandy.)

Reviewing the Facts of the Case

1. What did Harry Dimmick believe Eddie Slovik had to do in order to avoid trouble in his life? (He believed Eddie had to meet and marry a good woman who would keep him out of trouble.)
2. What was the 28th Division's nickname? Why was it given? (It was known as the "Hard Luck Division" because it seemed always to be involved in the fiercest battles of the war.)
3. Briefly describe the details of Eddie's two desertions. (In his first desertion, he remained behind his unit and stayed with the Canadian soldiers. In his second desertion, he ran away from his unit even after being told it was a serious military crime.)
4. How were deserters usually punished? (They were usually kept in jail and eventually released.)

5. What advice did General Eisenhower receive about Eddie's case? (He was advised that the death penalty should be carried out.)
6. What message did the commander of the 109th Infantry give his men after Eddie's execution? (He told his men that they did not have a right to life if they were unwilling to fight or even die for their country.)

Analyzing Ethical Issues

The following are possible duties associated with the stated constitutional rights:

1. The right to vote implies a duty to become informed on issues and to vote.
2. The right to religious freedom implies a duty to tolerate the religions of others.
3. The right to jury trials implies a duty to serve as a juror when called.

The following are possible duties associated with the claimed right:

1. Being permitted to drive implies a duty to drive with care.
2. Freedom to select one's neighborhood implies a duty to permit others to do so as well.
3. The right to use public parks implies a duty to avoid vandalizing the facilities so that others may enjoy them.

Expressing Your Reasoning

1. Was it wrong to execute Private Slovik? (The following are some considerations which might be raised favoring the execution: He had knowingly deserted after being warned; it might help prevent others from doing the same; his failure to fight might have contributed to the death of other soldiers who were fighting. Possible reasons against the execution: No others had been executed since the Civil War; other soldiers might think it too harsh; he would not have been a useful soldier on the front line but could have helped elsewhere.)
2. Writing assignment: Why do you disagree with this opinion about Eddie Slovik? (Students choose one opinion from the list in 2.a–2.d on student text page 186. In discussing students' essays, you may wish to determine which opinions students disagreed with. Students who disagreed with the same opinion can read their essays and compare the similarities and differences among their disagreements.)

ATOMIC FALLING-OUT
J. Robert Oppenheimer

Historical Understanding

1. What was meant by the term *fellow traveler*? (A fellow traveler is a person who supports some Communist causes but is not an official member of the Communist party.)
2. What was the Manhattan Project? (It was the code name for the secret effort to create an atomic bomb.)
3. What was one thing that Soviet leader Stalin did that led some Americans to turn away from their interest in communism? (Stalin signed a nonaggression treaty with Hitler. He also engaged in many brutal practices toward Soviet citizens.)

Reviewing the Facts of the Case

1. What did Chevalier tell Oppenheimer in their famous kitchen conversation? (Chevalier told Oppenheimer that George Eltenton had ways of getting secrets to the Russians. Oppenheimer said he would have nothing to do with it.)
2. What lie did Oppenheimer tell to security officials? (He told them that an acquaintance had contacted three scientists who were working on the bomb project and told them he could get secrets to the Russians.)
3. Why were security officials suspicious of Oppenheimer? (Oppenheimer had many friends, some of whom were Communists or fellow travelers. His wife had once been a Communist.)
4. After Hiroshima, what did Oppenheimer say to President Truman? How did the president react? (He told Truman, "Mr. President, I have blood on my hands." The president told an advisor that he did not want to see Oppenheimer again. The president said that he was the individual most responsible for the bombing because he had ordered it.)
5. What was the *super*? (It was the nickname for the hydrogen bomb.)
6. What were three reasons Oppenheimer was judged to be a security risk? (He had associated with Communists, he had delayed and lied in reporting the Chevalier conversation, and he lacked enthusiasm for the hydrogen bomb project.)
7. What shocked Chevalier when he heard the details of Oppenheimer's security hearing? (Oppenheimer had lost his security clearance and had given Chevalier's name to security officials.)

Analyzing Ethical Issues

The following questions are either factual or ethical:

1. Are people who sympathize with communism likely to give secrets to the Soviet Union? (Factual.)
2. Would Japan have surrendered if a demonstration nuclear blast were set off? (Factual.)
3. Was it right for Oppenheimer to withhold Chevalier's name from security officials? (Ethical.)
4. Did Chevalier lose important jobs because of Oppenheimer? (Factual.)

Expressing Your Reasoning

1. Should Oppenheimer have revealed Chevalier's name when first asked who told him about Eltenton? (In discussing student responses, consider the list of arguments 2.a–2.h on student text page 199. You may wish to emphasize the conflict between loyalty to a friend and the duty to uphold national security.)
2. Which arguments in favor of Oppenheimer's withholding of Chevalier's name are strong and which are weak? (Refer again to the list of arguments in the student text. Most students will be able to identify some reasons as more persuasive than others. They often have difficulty, however, articulating criteria that lie behind their selection of one reason over another. Establishing such criteria requires a sophisticated intellectual effort in ethical philosophy. It is unreasonable to expect students to pursue the ethical adequacy of reasons in great depth. They can, however, be introduced to the general problem of seeking criteria for justification.

   After students have identified some reasons as better than others, they should be asked to explain why they made their selections. After eliciting their explanations, you may wish to list the following ways in which reasons may be characterized:

   A reason that emphasizes revenge against an offending party
   A reason that stresses the self-interest of one party in the dispute
   A reason that stresses the need to show compassion for one or more of the parties involved
   A reason that emphasizes following custom or tradition
   A reason that shows respect for legitimate authority

A reason that shows concern for the welfare of society as a whole
A reason that attempts to take into account the rights of all parties concerned

Students may be asked if any of the above characterizations fit the reasons they selected. You may then discuss whether some of these types of reasons should be preferred over others. For example: Is a reason that shows respect for the rule of law better than one that focuses on revenge?)

3. Writing assignment: Was Oppenheimer right in advising that the bomb be used without warning? (In discussing students' paragraphs, see the two lists of arguments favoring and opposing the dropping of the bomb in 3.a–3.d on student text pages 199–200.)
4. Did Oppenheimer have an obligation to tell Chevalier he had given his name? (Some considerations for discussing whether or not Oppenheimer had an obligation to tell Chevalier he had informed on him are: He might have warned his friend to expect trouble; he might lose Chevalier as a friend; there had been no promise of confidentiality in the kitchen conversation; if Chevalier was really a spy and learned he was a suspect, he might destroy evidence; Chevalier had warned Oppenheimer about Eltenton.)

PINK LADY
Helen Gahagan Douglas

Historical Understanding

1. Identify the following: *The Marshall Plan, NATO, HUAC,* and the *Truman Doctrine.* (The Marshall Plan was a U.S. aid program for rebuilding ravaged economies of Western European countries following World War II. NATO, the North Atlantic Treaty Organization, is a postwar military alliance among Western European countries, Canada, and the United States designed to contain Soviet expansion in Europe. HUAC, the House Un-American Activities Committee, was a committee of the U.S. House of Representatives designed to investigate Americans suspected of disloyalty to the country. The Truman Doctrine was a policy of the Truman administration to provide military aid to Greece and Turkey to prevent them from falling under Soviet control.)

2. What was the *cold war*? (The cold war refers to combat without open fighting after World War II between the Soviet Union and the United States. It was accompanied by strong feelings of anticommunism within the United States.)
3. What three events in 1949 heightened fear of communism in the United States? (Alger Hiss, distinguished U.S. diplomat, was convicted of perjury for lying about giving government secrets to Communist agents. The Soviet Union exploded its first atom bomb. Chinese Communists took control of mainland China.)
4. What was *McCarthyism*? (Named after Senator Joseph McCarthy of Wisconsin, the term refers to accusing people recklessly of being Communists or Communist sympathizers, a frequent practice in the United States during the 1950s.)

Reviewing the Facts of the Case

1. Cite three positions taken by Helen Douglas that earned her a reputation as a liberal. (Civilian control of atomic energy; slum clearance and public housing; expanded social security; public ownership of power utilities; federal control of off-shore oil; expanded civil rights for members of minority groups.)
2. Why was there conflict between Helen Douglas and the Truman administration over UNRRA? (Douglas supported giving food and medical assistance to all needy people in postwar Europe. The Truman administration decided to restrict such aid to noncommunist nations.)
3. Why did Douglas vote against the Truman Doctrine? (She did not want the United States to act alone in blocking Soviet expansion. She preferred that Soviet threats in Greece and Turkey be blocked by the United Nations.)
4. For what reasons did Helen Douglas oppose the McCarran Internal Security Bill? Why did some of her colleagues in the House urge her to vote for the bill? (She opposed the bill because she believed it gave the government too much power and endangered the freedoms of speech, press, and assembly protected by the First Amendment. Colleagues urged her to vote for the bill because Richard Nixon might use a "no" vote to accuse her of being soft on communism. The bill was going to pass by a large margin anyway and, in any case, the bill would be vetoed by President Truman.)
5. How was the "pink sheet" used during the 1950 U.S. Senate campaign in California? (It was distributed by the Nixon campaign to leave the impression with voters that Helen Douglas had formed an alliance with

Vito Marcantonio, a procommunist Congressman from New York. The "pink sheet" also was intended to pin the label "Pink Lady" on Helen Douglas.)

Analyzing Ethical Issues

Which value(s) is (are) involved in each issue? Which of the positions stated for each issue is a liberal one and which is a conservative one?

1. Under whose control should the California oil tidelands be placed? (Values involved are authority and liberty.)
   a. Federal control of off-shore oil deposits is necessary to ensure that energy wealth is shared by all people in the country. (Liberal.)
   b. State governments know best how to manage resources within their boundaries. (Conservative.)

2. Should the Communist party be outlawed in the United States? (Value involved is liberty.)
   a. Communists intend to destroy democracy, and the United States should not tolerate forces bent on the destruction of its government. (Conservative.)
   b. In a democracy all are entitled to join the political party of their choosing, however unpopular its doctrines. (Liberal.)

3. Should the government pay for construction of public housing for poor people in slums? (Value involved is property).
   a. Some people can't afford the cost of good housing, but they still deserve a decent place to live. Those who can afford it should be taxed to help those in need. (Liberal.)
   b. People are responsible for housing themselves according to what they can afford to purchase. It is unfair to tax one person to pay someone else's rent. (Conservative.)

Expressing Your Reasoning

1. Should Helen Douglas have voted yes on the McCarran Internal Security Bill? (Reasons opposing her voting for the bill include: President Truman opposed the bill; it would violate her conscience to vote for the bill; the bill threatened civil liberties. Reasons favoring her voting for the bill include: It would provide the government tools to fight communism; support for the bill would help her political campaign; as head of the California Democratic ticket for the fall elections, she should try to avoid unpopular stands that might jeopardize the election of other California Democrats; the bill was going to pass by a large margin regardless of her vote; a presidential veto was expected if the bill was passed by Congress.

To pursue this further, students can be asked to ponder the issue, originally raised in Britain by Edmund Burke, of whether or not an elected legislator has a duty to vote the wishes of one's constituents when they conflict with one's conscience.)

2. Writing assignment: One of Richard Nixon's political advisors told the candidate that politicians must be willing and able to "shoot a little dirty pool." Was Nixon wrong to try and win the Senate seat in California by convincing voters that Helen Douglas was a communist sympathizer? (In discussing students' written statements, you may wish to pose reasons both favoring and opposing Nixon's tactics. Reasons in support of Nixon's campaign tactics include: Some foul play in politics is expected by the voters in elections—"Nice guys finish last"; it is all right to make one's opponent look as bad as possible during a political campaign; the communist threat required extraordinary measures to elect vigorous anticommunists. Reasons opposing Nixon's campaign tactics include: He stirred up excessive fears of communism; democratic government depends upon high standards of honesty by public officials; the charges against Douglas damaged her reputation; if deceit becomes acceptable in political compaigns, nothing said by candidates will be credible.)
3. Whether the candidates were truthful became a major issue during the 1950 Senate race in California. Each of the situations below involves the value of telling the truth. Indicate for each whether the truth ought to be told, and state a reason for your position. (A possible reason both for and against being truthful is presented for each situation.)
   a. Should a student tell the teacher about a classmate's cheating on the final exam? (For: If cheating on tests is tolerated, those who are dishonest and possibly incompetent will be placed in positions of authority. Against: Friends shouldn't get each other into trouble.)
   b. Should an intelligence agent tell a reporter about an assassination plot against a foreign official? (For: Citizens have a right to know when their government is engaged in questionable practices. Against: Spying requires total secrecy and extreme measures to protect national security.)
   c. Should a friend tell of plans for a surprise party when asked about them by the one to be surprised? (For: Friends should be truthful to maintain trust. Against: The surprise would be ruined.)
   d. During a trial, a lawyer discovers that her client committed the crime as charged. Should she tell the jury? (For: Evidence to convict those who commit criminal acts should not be withheld. Against: Lawyer-client communications are confidential, and proof of guilt is the prosecution's burden.)

e. Should a paid informant tell the police about a crime committed by his friend? (For: An informant should honor his agreement to supply police with information in exchange for money. Against: The informant will be considered untrustworthy by his friends.)

f. Should a middle-aged movie star tell the truth about her age? (For: Someone who tells lies will not be trusted by others. Against: "Little white lies" are expected and harmless.)

g. When asked, should a relative tell a terminally ill patient about his diagnosis? (For: People are entitled to know the truth about their own health. Against: One should protect loved ones from news that might be very upsetting.)

h. Should a spy reveal his true identity when questioned by enemy officials? (For: Deceiving people can destroy their faith in others. Against: Lying about one's identity is an expected part of a spy's work.)

i. Should a friend tell his buddy that his girlfriend was seen on a date with someone else? (For: A person is entitled to know when someone is breaking an agreement. Against: People are entitled to have private relationships that are kept secret.)

j. A young man dislikes his girlfriend's expensive new shoes. Should he admit it if she asks his opinion? (For: We should assume that someone who asks a question wants an honest answer. Against: Tact requires that we don't say things that may hurt others' feelings.)

A CLASH OF SYMBOLS
Paul Robeson

Historical Understanding

1. Identify two forms of discrimination faced by blacks during the first half of the twentieth century. (Among the forms of discrimination were refusal of service at certain restaurants and hotels and being separated from white passengers on passenger trains.)
2. What was the Harlem Renaissance? (A term applied to a time in Harlem when there was an unusual flourishing of black artists, writers, musicians, and intellectuals all living and working in the same area.)
3. What was the Truman Doctrine? (In March 1947, Truman said it would be United States policy to provide foreign aid to countries threatened by communist revolution.)

Reviewing the Facts of the Case

1. When he was a little boy, what advice about dealing with white people did Paul receive from his brother Reed? from his father? (His brother often fought with insulting whites and told Paul to hit them back harder than they hit him. His father opposed violence. He urged Paul to achieve the highest possible goals and always to act grateful to whites, never making whites fear him.)
2. Why was Paul's role in O'Neill's play controversial? (He portrayed a black man married to a white woman. Interracial marriage was illegal in many states and disapproved of in most places.)
3. What were two ways that Robeson's European travels influenced his thinking about racial issues? (He learned of the rich history and culture of Africa and became convinced that Americans needed to learn more about Africa. He was told that the Soviet Union opposed discrimination by race or sex.)
4. Why wouldn't Robeson sing at the Finnish benefit? (He was unwilling to protest the Soviet invasion of Finland.)
5. How did Robeson help the Allies during the war? (He spent a great deal of time and energy entertaining troops and workers in war industries as well as helping raise money for the war effort.)
6. What were two reasons Robeson was disappointed with President Truman? (He believed the president's foreign policy was extreme in its anti-Soviet Union stance, and he believed the president was failing to speak out strongly against racial violence in the United States.)
7. What did Robeson say at the Paris meeting that caused controversy in the United States? (The remarks that led to controversy in the United States were his claims that American blacks should not fight in a war with the Soviet Union.)
8. Why was Robeson's passport revoked? (Because of Robeson's many speeches criticizing United States policy, including objection to the Korean War, the State Department said it would not be in the interests of the United States to allow him to travel abroad.)

Analyzing Ethical Issues

The following incidents involved the values of liberty and loyalty:

1. Robeson refused to sing for the Finnish benefit. (There was the issue of his liberty to perform where he chose and to speak as he wished. There was also the issue of whether his primary loyalty was to the United States or to the Soviet Union in the Finnish controversy.)

2. When testifying before a committee in Washington, D.C., Robeson refused to answer the question of whether or not he was a member of the Communist party. (There was the issue of whether he should have the liberty to speak or not to speak regarding his political affiliations. There was also the issue of whether loyalty to the government required that he answer questions posed by the committee. Many people regarded refusal to answer the questions as automatic evidence of disloyalty.)

Expressing Your Reasoning

1. Should Robeson have returned to Peekskill for the September concert? (You may wish to ask students to consider the following reasons in favor of returning: It was a symbolic act against the violent protesters; he was invited to return; he wanted to raise money for an organization he supported; he had democratic ideas about freedom of assembly. Among the best reasons not to return, you may wish to ask students to consider: The likelihood of more violence; the fact that many local residents resented him; he might be hurting his cause by returning; he might be able to raise money by holding a concert elsewhere.)
2. While testifying before a committee in Washington, Robeson refused to answer the question of whether or not he was a Communist. Should he have answered the question? (In discussing whether Robeson should have answered the committee's question as to his communist affiliation you may wish to raise the following considerations in the discussion: He had once testified that he was not a Communist; by refusing to answer, people might think he was a Communist anyway; many people faced prison sentences for failing to answer the question; it was a controversial point whether or not the governmental committees had a right to inquire into people's political views.)
3. Writing assignment: Should Robeson's passport have been revoked by the State Department in 1950? (In considering whether or not the government should have revoked Robeson's passport you may wish to have students consider: Whether foreign travel is a right or a privilege; whether Robeson had an obligation to support U.S. policies when he was abroad; the fact that the Korean War was going on. In considering if he should have signed the document stating whether or not he was a Communist, the answers in question two above would apply as well as the fact that he had a concert tour that had to be canceled. Robeson's once substantial income was suffering because of his controversial statements. You may wish to ask students if his financial situation should have been a factor in his decision.)

SKY WARS
U-2 Episode

Historical Understanding

1. Why did the United States pursue a policy of *containment*? (The policy was intended to control the spread of communism.)
2. What does the term *cold war* mean? (It refers to a time of hostility between the Soviet Union and the United States when relations were strained, but actual military conflict was not occurring.)
3. Why did *Sputnik* cause concern among many Americans? (The successful launching of Sputnik caused Americans to fear the Soviet Union had a major lead in the space race and might even use satellite weapons to attack the United States.)

Reviewing the Facts of the Case

1. What did Eisenhower hope to accomplish by his Open Skies Plan? (He hoped the policy would reduce the chances of surprise attacks and lead to a relaxation of tension between the two nations.)
2. How did John Foster Dulles respond to Eisenhower's worries about the U–2? (Dulles said Eisenhower's worries were unfounded and that the Soviets would not admit an inability to detect the flights.)
3. What was one way the U–2 photographs were valuable to the United States? (They permitted knowledge of Soviet military developments and allowed the president to make informed judgments about the extent to which the United States should invest in defense.)
4. What cover story did the United States give after Khrushchev's first announcement of the downing of the U–2? (The United States claimed that the U–2 was a weather plane that had gone off course.)
5. Why did Allen Dulles offer to resign? (Dulles thought his resignation would take the blame for the incident away from Eisenhower.)
6. What was one reason President Eisenhower took personal responsibility for the U–2 missions? (He did not wish to seem out of control of the government.)
7. What were Khrushchev's demands of Eisenhower at Paris? How did the president respond? (He demanded cessation of the flights and an apology. Eisenhower said the flights had been canceled already and he would not crawl on his knees to meet any demands.)

8. What were two of Senator Fulbright's criticisms of the president? (He said that the president had violated diplomatic tradition and had used faulty reasoning in defending the spying.)
9. What did Francis Gary Powers' lawyer tell him to do? (He said Powers should cooperate, apologize, and admit his guilt.)
10. Why were many Americans critical of Powers? (Some Americans thought that he should not have given any information and should even have committed suicide.)

Analyzing Ethical Issues

Suggest one or two possible motives for the following actions (behaviors):

1. The State Department first claimed the downed U-2 was a weather plane. (A possible motive was that the State Department wanted to avoid being accused of spying.)
2. President Eisenhower would not meet Khrushchev's demands at Paris. (A possible motive was that Eisenhower wanted to appear strong and not cowardly or his belief that the demands were unreasonable.)
3. Khruschev made demands on Eisenhower at Paris. (A possible motive was that Khruschev wanted to embarrass Eisenhower or he wanted to end the Paris conference.)
4. Powers confessed to being a spy. (A possible motive was that Powers wanted to avoid punishment.)
5. Senator Fulbright criticized the president. (A possible motive was that Fulbright wanted to make the president look bad for political reasons or he was acting on the basis of true commitments.)

Expressing Your Reasoning

1. Should Eisenhower have apologized to Khruschev? (Some considerations favoring the apology that might be raised in discussing this question are: It might keep the peace conference alive; the United States had violated diplomatic tradition and should admit it; the apology might reduce cold war tensions. Opposing the apology: The president should not appear to give in to the Soviet Leader; there were many Soviet spies in the United States; the president should not appear weak.)
2. Should the president have allowed the State Department to release the cover story denying that the U-2 was on a spy mission? (In discussing this issue, some possible considerations that favor the release of the story are: No one knew for sure that the plane had not been completely destroyed; it is common practice for diplomats to release cover stories;

America's allies might have believed the story, and thus would have thought the United States had done nothing wrong. Considerations against the release of the story: It was too risky; the president might appear courageous for telling the truth; government leaders, like everyone else, have an obligation to tell the truth.)

3. Writing assignment: In a short speech, respond to Fulbright's criticisms of the president. (In discussing students' speeches, you may wish to make certain that both of the Senator's criticisms have been addressed: 1) diplomatic tradition had been broken and future diplomacy would be difficult, and 2) as a moral leader, the president should not claim that the need for information justified either secret methods for getting such information or the violation of Soviet airspace.)
4. Writing assignment: In a letter to the editor of *Newsweek* magazine, express an opinion about whether Powers should have used the poison pin. (In discussing students' letters, you may wish to raise the following considerations: Powers was not under orders to use the pin; the Soviets had the spy plane equipment and could tell that it was not a weather plane whether Powers lived or not; in taking the pin with him Powers might be said to have accepted the idea of using it; by using the pin, he could have avoided possible coercion that could have led him to divulge secret information.)

Volume 2, Part 4
SEARCHING FOR CONSENSUS
1961 to the Present

ROCK SMITES MOSES
Robert Moses

Historical Understanding

1. What is *urban sprawl*? (During the 1950s and 1960s, more and more people chose to live in outlying suburbs miles away from the inner city, even though they continued to hold jobs in the inner city. Improved highways, more automobiles, and to some extent, improved mass transportation contributed to urban sprawl.)
2. What is political *patronage*? (It is the practice of awarding government jobs to political supporters, rather than choosing the most qualified person for the job regardless of his or her political preferences.)
3. How are bonds used to finance major public projects? (People or organizations buy the special bonds. The money is used to build the project. In return, the bondholders, over a set period of time, get back their money plus a set rate of interest.)

Reviewing the Facts of the Case

1. Why did Robert Moses become a public hero? (More than any other person, Moses was responsible for creating an unprecedented number of public facilities for the people. His playgrounds, parks, and beaches met a genuine public need. In addition, he was seen as a man above dirty politics—one who was selflessly devoted to the public good.)
2. What were three of the ways Moses obtained power? (Some of the ways Moses gained power were the granting of political appointments, the shaping of laws that gave him authority, the use of secret files, the threat of resignation if people stood in his way, and the transformation of bond agreements into contracts, thus assuring the continued existence of the Triborough Bridge Authority.)
3. What was the Triborough Bridge Authority? Name one way it raised money for projects. (The Authority was established to build the Tri-

borough Bridge. Money was obtained through the issuance of bonds, and later through the use of tolls.)

4. In what way did Moses use the Constitution to maintain his power? (Article I, Section 10, of the United States Constitution prohibits states from interfering with the terms of legal contracts. The Triborough bond agreements were legal contracts and Moses had made part of their terms to be the continuance of the Triborough Authority.)
5. What was the "Battle of Central Park"? How did it affect Moses' reputation? (Moses attempted to build a parking lot in an area of the park that was loved by nearby residents. The residents attempted to stop the construction by placing their bodies in front of the construction equipment and later by going to court. Moses attempted to build the parking lot by sneaking the equipment in under cover of darkness. The bad publicity forced him to back down. His reputation suffered because he was now seen as something of a bully, no longer as protector of parks.)
6. Why did Governor Nelson Rockefeller want to strip Moses of his power? (Rockefeller wanted to get control of the Triborough money so that he could build mass transportation.)
7. What promise is it believed Governor Rockefeller made to Moses in order to gain his support for the MTA? (Apparently Rockefeller promised Moses a position of power in the new authority if he would support it.)

Analyzing Ethical Issues

Decide whether you consider each of the statements in the list below as illustrating an end or a means, and explain your reasoning. (What is important in this exercise is not whether students answer "ends" or "means," but how they explain their choices. Following each statement below is a possible correct response.)

1. Robert Moses learned how to get laws passed. (This can be seen as an *end*, the means for which was becoming Smith's aide in studying existing state laws and the law-making process. Getting laws passed can also be seen as a *means*, the end of which was to gain power so that projects could be built.)
2. Moses built the Triborough Bridge. (This can be seen as an *end*, the means for which were getting his appointment or pursuing bonds, and so forth. It may also be seen as a *means*, the end of which could be described as improving traffic flow, gaining public recognition, and so forth.)
3. Moses had special terms written into the Triborough bond agreements. (This is apparently a *means*, the end of which was to secure the continuance of the Triborough Authority so that more projects could be built.)

4. Governor Nelson Rockefeller expanded the state university system in New York. (This could be seen as a *means*, the end of which might be easier access to higher education for New York citizens. It may also be seen as an *end*, the means for which was reallocation of state funds.)
5. Moses tried to extend the parking lot of a restaurant in Central Park. (This can be seen as an *end*, the means for which were his efforts to quickly and secretly get the lot done. It may also be seen as a *means*, the end of which could be described as cementing his friendship with the restaurant owner, as easing parking problems, and so forth.)
6. Moses tried to eliminate political patronage from public employment in New York City. (This could be seen as a *means*, the end of which was more efficient government. It may also be seen as an *end*, a fair thing to do, the means for which were efforts to persuade political leaders to approve his plan.)

Expressing Your Reasoning

1. Would it have been right for Governor Rockefeller to have broken his promise to give Moses a position of power? (Among the reasons to be considered for Rockefeller's keeping his promise might be: The value of keeping promises should be upheld; Moses might hurt Rockefeller's reputation if he told the public that the governor could not be trusted; Moses might be a useful member of the MTA; Moses kept his end of the deal by helping persuade the public to vote for the MTA. Among the reasons to be considered for Rockefeller's breaking of the promise might be: Moses was no longer serving the public good because he opposed mass transportation; Rockefeller did not put his promise in writing; Moses had often played tough power politics in the past, and Rockefeller just gave him the same treatment.)
2. Which means employed by Moses are justified and why? (See the list of means Moses used, 2.a–2.e on student text pages 249–250. In discussing what aspects of means might be acceptable, students may be asked to consider the following: Was anyone hurt by the means? Were anyone's rights violated by the means? Were the ends vitally important? Were any laws broken? Did the means involve violating commonly agreed upon moral rules against lying, cheating, or breaking promises? Are the ends affected by the means?)
3. Writing assignment: How would you answer Moses' question: "If the end doesn't justify the means, what does?" (In discussing students' essays, you may wish to raise the following considerations: Aren't some means so reprehensible—for example, torture—that they should not be used regardless of the end intended? Can an end be said to be good if it is reached

by an unjustifiable means? Are some ends so important—for example, preservation of human life—that virtually any means would be justified in pursuing them?)

WHAT A WASTE
My Lai, Vietnam

Historical Understanding

1. How was the *domino theory* applied to Southeast Asia? (It was believed that if communism in Vietnam could not be stopped then neighboring nations would soon fall to communism.)
2. What was the *NLF*? (The National Liberation Front was an organization of South Vietnamese who were determined to overthrow the government by force.)
3. What was the *Gulf of Tonkin Resolution*? (Passed by the U.S. Congress, it gave the president the authority to use widespread military action in Southeast Asia.)
4. Why did the body count of enemy dead become a measure of the success of the war effort? (No clear battle lines existed, so progress could not be measured by the movement of battle lines. The number of enemy dead became the measure of success.)

Reviewing the Facts of the Case

1. What is a *free-fire zone*? What is a *search-and-destroy mission*? (A free-fire zone is an area that civilians are moved out of. It is then assumed that anyone remaining in the area is an enemy and can be fired upon. A search-and-destroy mission involves soldiers sweeping through an area seeking the enemy and attempting to kill them or take them prisoner.)
2. Identify three causes of danger to rural civilians during the war. (Rural civilians were endangered because U.S. troops often could not tell the difference between innocent civilians and the enemy, they were terrorized by NLF forces, and often they would not leave declared free-fire zones because of their attachment to their villages.)
3. What orders was Captain Ernest Medina said to have given to his soldiers? (His men were to burn My Lai, kill animals, and blow up escape tunnels.)
4. Describe the official military report of the results of My Lai. (It was reported as a successful operation in which 128 Vietcong were killed.)

5. What are three provisions of military law regarding the treatment of civilians during wartime? (Civilians are not to be killed, officers are not to order such killings, soldiers are not to obey such orders, and reports of such killings are to be investigated and wrongdoers are to be punished.)
6. Why were military men sometimes reluctant to report or investigate war crimes? (They sometimes believed the bad publicity would hurt the war effort or have a bad effect on their careers.)
7. What did Ronald Ridenhour's friends advise him about reporting what he knew about My Lai? What reasons did Ridenhour give for his reporting? (His friends told him not to report what he knew about My Lai. He said those who did wrong should be punished because their actions reflected on him and the ideals of the United States.)
8. Of what crime was Lieutenant William Calley convicted? (Calley was convicted of the murder of civilians.)

Analyzing Ethical Issues

The following questions are either factual or ethical:

1. Did most Americans support the war? (Factual.)
2. Could Ho Chi Minh have persuaded the NLF to seek peace? (Factual.)
3. Was it right to place William Calley on trial for murder? (Ethical.)
4. Did Captain Ernest Medina order his troops to kill villagers? (Factual.)
5. Should the United States have provided aid to the French? (Ethical.)
6. Was President Lyndon Johnson right in sending more troops to Vietnam? (Ethical.)
7. Would a North Vietnamese victory cause neighboring countries to become communist? (Factual.)
8. Did most South Vietnamese support the NLF? (Factual.)

Expressing Your Reasoning

1. Should Calley have been tried? (Among the reasons favoring the trial which you may wish students to consider are: Military law required it; the United States would look bad if no trials were held; wrong had been done and those responsible should be brought to justice. Reasons opposing the trial might be: There were other events like My Lai that

were not investigated nor were those involved tried; he may have been following orders; many Americans opposed the trial.)

2. Writing assignment: Should Ridenhour have reported My Lai? (In discussing students' paragraphs, you may wish to raise the following considerations: His friends opposed reporting; his former teacher favored reporting; it appeared no one else was going to do anything about it; he had not witnessed what happened; he believed the people involved should be punished.)

FINGERPRINCE
Robert Leuci and Police Corruption

Historical Understanding

1. What was the French Connection case? (The French Connection case refers to the breakup of a major drug ring that was bringing large amounts of narcotics into the United States from France.)
2. What is an *indictment*? (An indictment is a formal, legal accusation of wrongdoing.)
3. What is *perjury*? (Perjury is lying while under oath.)

Reviewing the Facts of the Case

1. Why were SIU detectives known as the Princes of the City? (The elite unit was regarded as a type of royalty within the New York City police force. They were envied and admired by other police officers and pursued their work without the usual supervision under which most police officers worked.)
2. Why was it difficult for government investigators to get proof of police corruption? (There was a code of loyalty among the police that kept them from informing on one another. In addition, accused criminals might claim to have evidence of police corruption, but their word was suspect.)
3. What deal did Nicholas Scoppetta make with Robert Leuci? (Scoppetta was a government investigator assigned to look into charges of police corruption. Leuci agreed to work with Scoppetta as long as he did not have to investigate his friends and partners. Also Leuci wanted to get evidence against corrupt lawyers and others, not simply to target police officers.)

4. What did Gina Leuci tell Robert when he was thinking about working with Scoppetta? (In essence she said that Leuci would not be able to control who got investigated and that eventually he would be forced to work against his friends and partners.)
5. Why was Leuci's family moved away from New York City? (They were moved for their protection. Officials had reason to believe that underworld figures suspected Leuci was involved in the investigations and that his family would be hurt or even killed.)
6. What perjury did Leuci commit? What was one reason he did it? (Under oath, Leuci denied having committed more than three illegal acts. He also denied having given drugs to addict informers. One reason he did it was to protect his friends and former partners. Another was to maintain his credibility with future juries. If he admitted to more than three acts of wrongdoing, he would be admitting that he had lied earlier when he said there were only three instances. Juries might then doubt his word when he was testifying against defendants.)
7. What did Carl Aguiluz tell government investigators? (He admitted that he and SIU detectives with whom he had worked had given drugs to informers, had taken money, and had given perjured testimony. He also claimed that Leuci had been involved in many illegal acts, although he did not have firsthand evidence against Leuci.)
8. What were two reasons it was difficult for Leuci to tell the truth to government investigators? (He did not want to break the bonds of silence and loyalty. He feared one or more of his friends might commit suicide as Nunziata had. He feared that he might be indicted if he confessed to illegal activities.)

Analyzing Ethical Issues

The following decisions involve factual and ethical issues:

One decision was whether Leuci should tell all the truth to the government investigators.
Some factual issues involved: Would he be indicted? Would any of his friends kill themselves? Would his past testimony be discredited?
Some ethical issues involved: Would it be right to inform on his partners? Did the general obligation to be truthful apply in this case?

Another decision was whether Leuci should be indicted.
Some factual issues involved: Would his past testimony be discredited? Would future juries believe government witnesses?

Some ethical issues involved: Did the government have an obligation to overlook his crimes because of the heroic work he accomplished? Should he be allowed to go free when others had been convicted of similar crimes?

Expressing Your Reasoning

1. Should Robert Leuci have told the truth about illegal activities in which he and his partners engaged? (Among the reasons for telling the truth, which you may wish students to consider, are: The general moral value of truth-telling; Leuci's apparent need to overcome his guilty conscience; a duty to expose the wrongdoing of his partners. Among the reasons for not telling the truth are: The extent of his obligations to his friends, the police officer's code of loyalty; the possibilities of indictment.)
2. Writing assignment: Should Leuci have been indicted? (In discussing students' paragraphs, among the reasons favoring his indictment, which you may wish students to consider, are: Crimes should be punished; the government needed to maintain an image of using truthful witnesses; others had been indicted for the same or similar crimes. Among the reasons against indicting him are: He had done heroic work; his past testimony against defendants might be overturned; he had suffered enough.)
3. Evaluate different situations in which secret recordings are made by police officers. (See the list of situations, 3.a–3.d on student text page 272. In discussing the situations, you may wish to have students consider the following: The motive for the recording, for example, personal animosity versus reasonable suspicion a crime will be discovered; the issue of whether the general societal need to fight crime justifies any of the forms of secret recording. Students may be interested in the following background information: Electronic eavesdropping by police is governed by interpretations of the Fourth Amendment protection against unreasonable search and seizure; to place a lawful wiretap, police must obtain a warrant from a judge, who must be persuaded that there is "probable cause" to believe evidence of criminal activity will be obtained; illegally obtained evidence may not be used in court under the exclusionary rule.

   Recently, there has been governmental discussion about modifying these current policies. You may wish to ask students their views of the exclusionary rule. For example, is justice served if criminal actions are not punished because of the rule?)

COVER-UP UNCOVERED
John Dean and Watergate

Historical Understanding

1. Identify three important foreign policy problems facing President Richard Nixon in the early 1970s. (Among the problems facing the president were easing Arab-Israeli tensions, ending the war in Vietnam, developing good relations with mainland China, and reducing the U.S.–Soviet tensions.)
2. What was unusual about the number of votes President Nixon received in 1972? (He received more votes than any other presidential candidate in history.)
3. What is *obstruction of justice*? (It is the crime of attempting to block or hinder a criminal investigation.)

Reviewing the Facts of the Case

1. What was the CRP? Who was John Mitchell? (The CRP was the Committee to Re-Elect the President. John Mitchell, former attorney general, headed the CRP during the time of the break-in.)
2. Immediately after the break-in, why did people suspect the burglars might be connected to the White House or the CRP? (The name Howard Hunt, who had worked at the White House, appeared on notes in the pockets of two of the burglars. One of the burglars had worked at the CRP.)
3. What job did H. R. Haldeman offer John Dean? What were two things that Dean realized he would have to do in order to get ahead? (Dean was offered the job of counsel to the president. To get ahead he would have to be loyal, do a good job, and keep silent about presidential discussions.)
4. Why would the president's chances for re-election be hurt if the truth of Watergate came out? (The public would probably be disgusted to find that the president's friends and top advisors were involved in committing a crime. It is likely the president himself would be suspected as well.)
5. What were two ways John Dean was involved in the cover-up? (Destroying evidence to hinder the FBI investigation and helping raise and pass money to the burglars hoping they would remain silent about the truth.)
6. In his August 1972 press conference, what did the president say about

Dean? (He announced that Dean had completed an investigation showing no White House involvement with the Watergate break-in. Dean had made no such investigation or report to the president.)

7. Who was James McCord? In what way did he expose the cover-up? (McCord was one of the convicted burglars. After the trial, he sent a letter to Judge Sirica saying that higher-ups had been involved. He also told investigators that Dean was involved.)
8. Why did Dean meet with the president on March 21, 1973? What were two things that were discussed? (Dean wanted to tell the president all the facts about Watergate, the cancer growing on the presidency. They discussed continuing to supply hush-money to the burglars, the writing of a phony Dean report, and the possibility of having top advisors resign and take the blame for Watergate.)

Analyzing Ethical Issues

Among the ethical questions involving truth and/or loyalty are:

Should Dean have resigned? This involves the value of Dean's loyalty to the president and the extent of his obligation to protect him.

Were the prosecutors right in telling Dean, falsely, that Liddy had been talking? This involves the value of truth. Were the prosecutors justified in lying to get the truth from Dean?

Should Dean have revealed the truth about Watergate? This involves both truth and loyalty in conflict: His professed loyalty to the president and his general obligation to tell the truth.

Expressing Your Reasoning

1. Should John Dean have told the truth about the Watergate affair? State reasons for your position. (Some reasons for Dean telling the truth, which you may wish your students to consider, are: Dean should protect himself by cooperating; Dean has a general obligation to tell the truth; someone else might tell on Dean; the strain of the cover-up was upsetting Dean and his relationship with his wife; he had been breaking the law. Some reasons against Dean telling the truth are: Dean had pledged his loyalty to the president and knew he was not to talk about things that the president had said; he had been involved in the cover-up and by talking he would probably go to jail; his telling the truth would cause a crisis in the nation and would hurt the president's ability to conduct foreign and domestic affairs; by telling the truth he would be hurting his friends.)

2. The president wanted John Dean to resign and, in effect, take the blame for Watergate. Should Dean have resigned? (In discussing this, you may wish to focus on the nature and extent of one's obligation of loyalty. Dean had frequently said that he was loyal and wanted to protect the president. Why should he not be willing to sacrifice himself to protect the president and his national and international credibility?)
3. Were the prosecutors right in telling Dean that Liddy had been talking with them? (Focus of discussion might well be on the general issue of means and ends. That is, are law officials right in lying so that they can determine the truth? You may wish to ask students to make a list of situations in which the truth is distorted or withheld to achieve some end, and ask them if it is justified in each situation. For example, a teenager knows his friend has shoplifted something but refuses to tell a store detective when the detective asks him if he knows who did the shoplifting.)
4. Writing assignment: Should President Gerald Ford have pardoned Nixon? (In discussing students' paragraphs, a variety of considerations may be raised. For example: The president resigned in disgrace and that was punishment enough; the president should not be treated any differently than the others who had to face trial and jail terms; the nation had enough trauma about Watergate, there was no need to pursue it further; all the criminals had been removed from power; putting a president on trial would be a bad precedent for our system of government; there was no good reason to pardon him, it might encourage future presidents to do illegal things.)

BUYING YOUR PARDON
Marie Ragghianti

Historical Understanding

1. What connection was there between the Watergate scandal and Ray Blanton's campaign for governor of Tennessee? (Blanton tried to associate his opponent with Watergate. The results of the Tennessee election, coming soon after Watergate, would be an indication of how much damage had been done by the scandal to the Republican party.)
2. Explain the meaning of the following: *extradition, grand jury indictment, executive clemency,* and *extortion.* (Extradition is the surren-

der of an alleged criminal by one government to another for trial. A grand jury is a group of citizens convened by a court to decide whether there is enough evidence to hold a suspect for trial. An indictment is a written accusation by a grand jury charging one or more persons with a crime. Executive clemency is reduction of a criminal's sentence by the head of a government. Extortion is the unlawful use of an official position to obtain something of value not due, usually money.)

Reviewing the Facts of the Case

1. How did Marie Ragghianti come to be appointed state extradition officer? (She was offered the post by Eddie Sisk, an acquaintance from the Democratic party.)
2. What was Eddie Sisk's official position in the Blanton administration? (Sisk was Governor Blanton's legal counsel.)
3. What hardships were eased for Ragghianti when she received her first state job? (The hardships of supporting her three children alone with little income were eased by the salary from her state job.)
4. What was the function of the Tennessee Board of Pardons and Paroles? (The Tennessee Board of Pardons and Paroles received requests for clemency from prisoners and made recommendations to the governor to grant or deny them.)
5. What steps did Ragghianti take once she suspected corruption in the state corrections system? (She raised her suspicions with the commissioner of corrections, a friend, the governor, and then the FBI.)
6. Why did Ragghianti feel guilty after reporting her suspicions of Sisk to the state commissioner of corrections and to the governor? (She felt guilty, because Eddie had helped her get her first state job and she considered him a friend.)
7. What key evidence was finally turned up by the FBI? (A witness testified that Sisk had taken a payoff. When he was arrested, he was carrying cash from a payoff.)

Analyzing Ethical Issues

Some of the factual issues raised in this story: Were the arrests of Ragghianti attempts to discredit her charges? Did Blanton lose his re-election attempt because of Ragghianti's charges? Did the governor know about all of Sisk's wrongdoings?

Some of the ethical issues raised in this story: Was it wrong to grant clemency to a prisoner because the prisoner's father had contributed money to Blanton's compaign? Should Ragghianti have reported her suspicions to the FBI? Should Ragghianti have been reappointed to the Board of Pardons and Paroles?

Expressing Your Reasoning

1. Should Marie Ragghianti have gone to the FBI with evidence that convicts were buying clemencies from the governor's office? (Reasons supporting Marie's decision include: She might be accused of participating in the scheme if it were discovered later; those involved should be exposed for violating the law and their oaths of office; the purpose of granting clemencies is to restore rehabilitated convicts to society, not to reward elected officials with money; those convicts released because of payoffs might still be dangerous; it is unfair to convicts who have no money to grant clemency to those who can afford to pay. Reasons opposing Marie's decision include: Her life might be in danger; by cooperating with those selling pardons, she could get some of the payoff money; by rocking the boat, she might lose her job and the security it provided her children; a scandal in the governor's office could tarnish the reputation of the Democratic party; she owed loyalty to Eddie Sisk.)
2. Eddie Sisk suspected that Ragghianti may have been the one who triggered the FBI raid on his office. When he questioned her about it, she denied it. Was it right for her to lie to him? (Reasons supporting Ragghianti's misleading Sisk include: If Sisk knew the truth, he might feel betrayed; Sisk might get angry at Ragghianti and retaliate; Sisk had not been honest with her; by concealing her involvement, Ragghianti might get more evidence for the FBI investigation. Reasons opposing Ragghianti's misleading Eddie include: She was lying to a friend; she owed him a debt for helping her get her job; she could help protect Sisk from prosecution by revealing to him what the FBI knew.)
3. Writing assignment: Should law enforcement officials offer suspects immunity deals in order to convict other suspects? (In discussing students' paragraphs, you may wish to raise reasons both for and against granting immunity to suspects in exchange for testimony. Some reasons in favor of the practice are: It makes police investigations easier; sometimes there is no other source of evidence; it increases the chances of conviction, thereby deterring other prospective criminals; it is better to convict some suspects than none. Some reasons against the practice are: Police should gather evidence without pressuring friends to be disloyal to each other; suspects may be dangerous and should not be freed in exchange for information; letting one suspect off is unfair to the others.)

4. One possible reason is presented both for and against accepting each job.

a. A man is hired as a teacher because he is a member of a minority group. (*Yes:* Minorities have been denied jobs in the past. *No:* A job offer should be accepted if based on one's merit as an individual and not on one's membership in a group.)

b. A woman is hired as a waitress because she has a shapely figure. (*Yes:* One should use all advantages in getting a desired job. *No:* It promotes sexist treatment.)

c. Someone is appointed to a vacancy in a legislature because his father was famous. (*Yes:* Leadership is sometimes a family tradition. *No:* People should benefit from their own achievements, not those of their parents.)

d. A job is offered to someone because of the applicant's political views. (*Yes:* Employers should be free to choose like-minded employees. *No:* Qualifications to perform the duties of a job should be the basis for employment, not someone's beliefs.

Note: Political beliefs might be a qualification to perform the duties of some jobs, for example, campaign manager. Also, you may wish to distinguish here between public and private employment.)

AFFIRMATIVE OR NEGATIVE
Bakke Decision

Historical Understanding

1. What purpose did the post-Civil War amendments to the Constitution have in common? (The Reconstruction amendments to the Constitution were designed to grant political rights to former slaves.)

2. At the turn of the century, what were two kinds of discrimination against blacks in the South? (At the turn of the century, most southern blacks were denied rights of citizenship. For example, they were not allowed to vote, were excluded from juries, and were prevented from holding public office. They were also segregated from whites by law; for example, they were required to attend separate schools, travel on separate railroad cars, and eat in separate restaurants.)

3. How was the U.S. Supreme Court precedent in *Plessy* v. *Ferguson* (1896) changed by its decision in *Brown* v. *Board of Education* (1954)? (Plessy established that separate facilities for the races were constitutional if they were equal. *Brown* reversed that precedent by declaring separate public schools inherently unequal and therefore unconstitutional.)

4. What were two events during the civil rights movement in which Martin Luther King was a leader? (Martin Luther King, Jr. led the 1955 Montgomery bus boycott and the 1963 march on Washington.)
5. What were three provisions of civil rights laws passed by Congress during the 1960s? (The Civil Rights laws of the 1960s outlawed discrimination in public accommodations, employment, and housing; authorized lawsuits for school integration; and removed restrictions on voting by blacks.)
6. What is the aim of *affirmative action*? (The aim of affirmative action is to increase participation of underrepresented minority groups in all areas of life in the United States.)

Reviewing the Facts of the Case

1. Briefly describe the special admissions program at the medical school of the University of California at Davis. (The Davis special admissions program reserved 16 of 100 places in its entering medical school class for disadvantaged minority students.)
2. What were Allan Bakke's main arguments against the Davis special admissions program? (Bakke claimed the special admissions program established an unconstitutional racial quota and allowed lower entrance standards for minority students than for whites.)
3. What were the major arguments of the university in defense of its special admissions program? (The university argued that the special admissions program was designed not to exclude anyone but to include minorities who had been denied admissions in the past. The university also claimed that the special program provided a diverse student body, reduced segregation of minorities in society, offered role models for minority children, and improved medical care in minority communities.)
4. What were two points made before the Supreme Court by the solicitor general of the United States in the Bakke case? (The solicitor general argued that the government must sometimes take race into account as a temporary step to achieve racial equality, that the effects of past discrimination required measures to bring blacks "up to the starting line," and that some minority students with lower grades and test scores may have as much potential to become doctors as whites with higher scores.)
5. How did Justice Powell strike a compromise in the Bakke decision? (Under Justice Powell's compromise, the university was ordered to admit Bakke and was permitted to take an applicant's race into account so long

as a rigid racial quota was not established. The justice thereby forged a majority decision by taking part of the conflicting opinions of the two disagreeing minorities on the Supreme Court.)

Analyzing Ethical Issues

Underrepresentation must be the result of intentional discrimination for it to be a violation of the Constitution. A way for each situation to have occurred with *no* intent to discriminate is presented first. Then, evidence that might establish an intent to discriminate is presented.

1. An elementary school is all white. (*No intent:* No blacks lived in the area. *Evidence of intent:* Blacks and whites lived near each other but were assigned to separate schools.)
2. Only Jewish people live in a large apartment building. (*No intent:* Friends and relatives rented in the same building. *Evidence of intent:* Apartments were refused to non-Jews who wanted to rent.)
3. All flight attendants working for an airline are female. (*No intent:* No males had applied. *Evidence of intent:* Applications were not accepted from males.)
4. A trade union has no Hispanic members. (*No intent:* There were no Hispanics holding jobs encompassed by the union. *Evidence of intent:* Hispanics held the same jobs as union members but were denied union membership.)
5. A public transportation system has no handicapped riders. (*No intent:* Transit officials overlooked the special needs of handicapped riders. *Evidence of intent:* Facilities for handicapped passengers were removed from the budget.)
6. A fast-food restaurant has only teenage employees. (*No intent:* Only teenagers applied for the jobs. *Evidence of intent:* Adult applicants were not hired.)

Expressing Your Reasoning

1. Should the medical school at the University of California-Davis have established a special admissions program for disadvantaged minority applicants? (Reasons supporting the university's special admissions program include: It would help correct past discrimination; it would increase black membership in the medical profession; it might improve medical care in minority communities; it would create racial diversity in the medical school; minority applicants have not had an equal opportu-

nity to compete on admissions tests. Reasons opposing the special admissions program include: Those admitted under the lower standards of the special program may be less qualified to practice medicine; race has nothing to do with competence to practice medicine; the program discriminates against qualified whites; minorities might come to believe they can succeed only when given preferential treatment.)

2. Affirmative action programs have been adopted in a variety of places. State whether or not you think each of the following plans is fair. Present reasons for your positions.
   a. The Detroit Police Department adopted a plan to promote equal numbers of black and white officers. (Reasons supporting and opposing the Detroit Police Department affirmative action program are similar to those presented for the Bakke case. In Detroit, however, past discrimination against blacks in promotion of police officers was acknowledged by the Police Department. The Detroit program was upheld by a federal appeals court, and in 1984 the Supreme Court declined to hear an appeal.
   b. Dade County, Florida, set aside 10 percent of its public works contracts for minority-owned firms. (In 1984, a federal appeals court upheld the Dade County plan. The U.S. Justice Department argued that the Constitution gives Congress special powers to fashion remedies for past discrimination, but that state and local governments have no authority to award contracts based on racial classifications. Dade County officials argued that there has been a lack of participation by blacks in the economic growth of the Miami area. The affirmative action plan, they claimed, would correct past and ongoing economic discrimination against blacks. The affirmative action program was established following civil unrest in the black Liberty City area of Miami. The U.S. Supreme Court refused to accept the case on appeal.
   c. The Kaiser Aluminum Company and the United Steelworkers of America voluntarily agreed to a plan to increase the number of black workers in skilled positions. (Unlike the other affirmative action programs presented, the Kaiser Aluminum plan in Louisiana involved an agreement between a private corporation and a trade union. It did not involve government action. The plan was challenged in court by Brian Weber, a white worker, who applied for but was denied a training program for skilled workers. Weber claimed the program unlawfully discriminated against him because of his race. Weber lost his case. The U.S. Supreme Court found that the Civil Rights Act was intended to improve job opportunities for minorities and that it did not prohibit a voluntary affirmative action plan designed to eliminate

a racial imbalance. As students present their own judgments in the affirmative action cases presented, you may want to ask whether those judgments are based on equal opportunity, equal treatment, or equal result.)

3. Writing assignment: Should Allan Bakke have been rejected by some medical schools because of his age? (In discussing students' short essays, you may wish to point out that a major reason supporting age restriction in medical school admissions is: The state has an interest in getting more years of medical practice from the students it educates. A major reason opposing is: Older applicants may bring valuable experience and maturity to the practice of medicine. To discuss the fairness of age discrimination in other contexts, you may want to raise the following considerations: Mandatory early retirement when physical fitness is an important job qualification, for example, a police officer's job; as a response to a high level of shoplifting, young people are allowed in a store only when accompanied by an adult; compulsory school attendance laws for youth; minimum age requirement for obtaining a driver's or marriage license; limits on the number of hours a young person can work on a job as exemplified by child labor laws.)

KING TO PAWN
Iranian Hostage Crisis

Historical Understanding

1. How did Shah Reza Pahlavi originally come to power in Iran? (He was placed in power by England and Russia early in World War II. These powers had invaded Iran to overthrow a pro-German government.)
2. What were two reasons that a stable, friendly Iran was believed important for U.S. interests? (A stable, friendly Iran was deemed important to the United States because Iran could protect the Persian Gulf and serve as a buffer against the Soviet Union.)
3. How did the United Nations, the International Court, and most nations of the world react to the embassy takeover? (All condemned the taking of hostages and urged that they be released.)
4. Why were many nations unwilling to admit the shah after he left Iran? (Any nation that admitted the shah would offend Iran, and economic or other forms of retaliation might be taken.)

Reviewing the Facts of the Case

1. What did the militant Iranians demand before they would release the hostages? (They demanded the return of the shah to Iran to face trials for his alleged crimes.)
2. Why did many Iranians despise the United States? (They believed the United States had, through the CIA, restored the shah to power in 1953. They also believed the United States had helped train SAVAK.)
3. Why did Iranian religious leaders oppose the shah's attempts to change Iran? (Religious leaders opposed his actions because they were seen as violating traditional Islamic beliefs and because they believed that western influences were immoral.)
4. How did Ayatollah Khomeini continue to influence events in Iran after he was expelled from the country? (Tape recorded messages from the ayatollah were smuggled into Iran. In his messages, he called for the overthrow of the shah.)
5. What were three policies enacted by the ayatollah when he gained power in Iran? (Women were ordered to wear the chador, the press was censored, summary trials and executions were held, and music and dancing were forbidden.)
6. How did President Jimmy Carter respond to the pro-Khomeini Iranians' request for a permit to demonstrate in front of the White House? (He denied the request for a permit.)
7. What were three things President Carter did to try to gain the release of the hostages? (He froze Iranian assets, canceled delivery of military parts to Iran, went to the United Nations and the International Court, and authorized the rescue mission.)

Analyzing Ethical Issues

Among the incidents or problems associated with the identified values are:

Authority: The ayatollah's refusal to obey the International Court.
Property: Carter's decision to freeze Iranian assets.
Liberty: Carter's denial of the permit to demonstrate.
Life: The decision to attempt the rescue mission.
Loyalty: Admitting the shah into the United States.

Expressing Your Reasoning

1. Should President Jimmy Carter have allowed Shah Reza Pahlavi into the United States for medical treatment? (You may wish to have your

students consider the following: the potential threat to Americans in Iran; the idea that the shah had long been an American ally; the notion that the United States often willingly admitted political refugees; the reputation of the shah as a brutal dictator; the medical reports of the shah's severe illness.)

2. Should the president have traded the shah for the hostages? (You may wish to have your students consider the following: The general problem of giving in to terrorists; the fact that the shah would probably have been tried and executed if he had returned to Iran; the fact that such a trade would have guaranteed that American lives would not be taken; the results of public opinion polls; whether people should ever be treated as bargaining items.)
3. Writing assignment: Should the president have ordered a military rescue attempt? (In discussing students' paragraphs, you may wish to raise the following considerations: whether all other possible efforts to free the hostages had been made; whether the forthcoming election should influence the president's decision; the possibility that some of the hostages might be wounded or killed in the rescue attempt.)

ABOUT THE AUTHORS

ALAN L. LOCKWOOD taught high-school United States history in Massachusetts. He received his B.A. degree, specializing in social studies, from Syracuse University. Both his master's and doctoral degrees are in education from Harvard University. He has written extensively about values education and is currently a professor of curriculum and instruction at the University of Wisconsin in Madison.

DAVID E. HARRIS taught junior- and senior-high-school United States history in Madison, Wisconsin. He also taught social studies education courses in Michigan at Oakland University and the University of Detroit. He received his B.A. degree in history and both his M.S. and Ph.D. degrees in social studies education from the University of Wisconsin. Currently, he is the social studies consultant at the Oakland Schools, an intermediate school district serving the local school districts of Oakland County, Michigan.